TRENDS AND CHALLENGES TO INDIAN BANKING

H.L. Sharma

RAJAT PUBLICATIONS
New Delhi

Trends and Challenges to Indian Banking
by *H.L. Sharma*

This edition is published by Rajat Publications
4740/23, Ansari Road Daryaganj,
New Delhi - 110002

ISBN: 978-81-7880-290-9

Edition 2025

Rs. 1395/-

Printed and bound in India

RAJAT
PUBLICATIONS

4740/23, Ansari Road, Daryaganj,
New Delhi- 110002 (India)
Mob:- +91-9811484973, +91-9811105389
E-mail: rajat_publication@yahoo.com

TO

MY REVEREND

PARENTS

ACKNOWLEDGEMENTS

In the completion of present research work, I have received generous help, guidance and co-operation from various quarters. It is difficult to recount all of them. I beg due apologies to all those, whose contribution I have not been able to recount. However, I can not afford not to mention a few. First and foremost, I owe an immense debt of gratitude to Dr (Mrs.) Meenakshi Sooden, Professor, Department of Economics, H.P.U. Shimla, who basically developed my interest in research and has been a perennial source of inspiration.

I have the rare privilege of getting encouragement from Professor Neelkantha Rath - the renowned economist of India. I am deeply indebted to him for sparing time from his valuable schedule and make suggestions relating to the methodology of the study.

It is a matter of utmost pleasure for me to express my indebtedness and gratitude to Dr L.R. Sharma (Ex-Chairman, Deptt. of Economic, H.P.U. Shimla), Dr M.R. Khurana (Ex-Chairman, Deptt. of Economics, Punjab University, Chandigarh), Dr Satish Verma (Chairman, Deptt. of Economics, G.N.D.U. Amritsar), Dr Burange (Professor, Deptt. of Economics, University of Mumbai), Dr Virender Kaundal (Assistant Professor, Deppt. of Economics, Jammu University) and Dr T. Raman Sharma (Sr. Lecturer, Govt. College Arki, H.P.), for their creative criticism, comments and valuable suggestions for the improvement in analysis.

I owe a life long debt to all the reverend and distinguished teachers, who taught me from the beginning of my studies, till now. I also express my regards to Prof. O.C. Malhotra, Principal and my friends & colleagues at Govt. P.G. College Mandi, for providing encouragement to carry out and complete the present work.

At this stage, I also acknowledge my thanks to all the scholars and researchers, spread over various books, journals, magazines and dailies, whose studies benefited me in writing the book. The generous help rendered by the librarians and the library staff of H.P.U. Shimla, Indian Institute of Advanced Study, Shimla, Directorate of Economics and Statistics, Shimla, Punjab University Chandigarh, University of Mumbai and I.C.S.S.R. Delhi, is worthy to be gratefully acknowledged.

Above all, I owe a life long debt to my revered parents, who have been providing me immeasurable love, affection, care and moral support. I express my profound gratitude and esteemed regards to them. I am immensely indebted to my loving grand mother for her blessings and care for me. I also owe a lot to my brothers, Dr R.P. Sharma & Mr D.C. Nadda, sisters-in-law, Dr(Mrs) Meenakshi & Mrs Aarti, who made valuable suggestions for the improvement and encouraged to carry out the research work.

My wife, Seema and sons, Harshit & Satvik deserve special appreciation and deep love for showing rare perseverance and providing all kinds of help and encouragement during the long period of research work.

Last but not least, I am thankful to the U.G.C. authorities for providing financial assistance to carryout the research project.

Notwithstanding, the shortcomings remained are my own responsibility.

HARBANS LAL SHARMA

PREFACE

Financial sector forms a very significant part of the infrastructure, which is essential for the development of a country. Among financial entities, commercial banks are the predominant financial intermediaries. In developing countries, the role of commercial banks is not confined to accepting of deposits and deploying of funds, but includes of accelerating the flow of credit in accordance with the national priorities and needs of economic development.

One of the important problems faced by the developing countries today, is the glaring disparities in the level of economic development and variations in the rates of growth of different regions within the country. The regional imbalances and lopsided growth of a country are not conducive to the national goal of balanced growth with stability and hence social justice. It is the fact that unregulated process of economic growth leading to regional disparities, results in numerous economic, social and political problems. It is therefore, rightly considered that the reduction in regional disparities is of utmost importance in the context of social justice, accelerated growth and maintaining national integration and unity. A more equitable distribution of income and wealth is essential not only to promote greater social justice, but also to improve economic efficiency, raise substantially the level of national income, output employment and social welfare.

The role of commercial banks in establishing an egalitarian society is very crucial and significant. They help in this direction by suitably designing their policies. By opening their branches in backward areas, banks make credit facilities available to the disadvantaged and socially important sectors. Also, the funds collected from developed regions, may be channelised for investment in underdeveloped regions of the country. In this way, they bring about more balanced regional development. In fact, since their nationalization, commercial banks in India, have been playing a pivotal role in achieving balanced regional development and contributing to the overall economic development of the country in the desirable form. With the coming up of many new market oriented policies, in the wake of financial sector reforms in India, the responsibilities of the scheduled commercial banks in reducing personal and regional disparities have increased many fold.

The present study seeks to examine the trends in regional disparities of commercial banking development in India, during the pre and post financial sector reform period. It comprises of five chapters in all. The *first chapter* has been divided into four sections. The first section brings into light the role of commercial banks in economic development of a country. A brief history of banking in India, has been discussed in second section. The third section, provides a bird's eye view of the financial sector reforms in India. Further, the fourth section has been devoted to exhibit the structure of banking system in India. In *second chapter*, a brief review of studies conducted earlier has been summarized. The *third chapter* outlines the research design in the form of need, scope, objectives, methodology, plan and limitations of the study. The *fourth chapter* has been divided into two sections. In the first section, the extent and direction of inter-state variations of commercial banking development in India has been examined. The second section analyses the impact of financial sector reforms on banking in India. Finally, the *last chapter* summarises the findings and conclusions of the study and points out some suggestions for healthy growth of banking.

Author

ABBREVIATIONS

Advs.	-	Advances
Agri.	-	Agriculture
AIFLs	-	All India Financial Institutions
AMR	-	Aggregate Monetary Resources
ANOVA	-	Analysis of Variance
Brs.	-	Branches
BSR	-	Basic Statistical Returns
CBs	-	Commercial banks
CCI	-	Controller of Capital Issues
CDR	-	Credit-Deposit Ratio
CFS	-	Committee on Financial System
CGC	-	Credit Guarantee Corporation
CLDB	-	Central Land Development Bank
Co.	-	Company
CRAR	-	Capital to Risk Weighted Asset Ratio
CRR	-	Cash Reserve Ratio
CV	-	Coefficient of Variation
DFIs	-	Development Financial Institutions
Deps.	-	Deposits
DIS	-	Deposit Insurance Scheme
DRI	-	Differential Rate of Interest
ed.	-	editor/edited

e.g.	-	exempli gratia(for example)
et. al.	-	et alli(and others)
etc.	-	etcetra
EPW	-	Economic and Political Weekly
FA	-	Factor Analysis
Fig.	-	Figure
FSS	-	Farmers Service Societies
GCA	-	Gross Cropped Area
GM	-	Geometric Mean
GOI	-	Government of India
Ha.	-	Hectare
HI	-	Herfindahl Index
ibid.	-	ibidem (in the same place or work)
IDBI	-	Industrial Development Bank of India
i.e.	-	id est (that is)
IPBN	-	Index of Penetration of Banking Network
IRDP	-	Integrated Rural Development Programme
Jr.	-	Journal
Kgs.	-	Kilograms
Km(s).	-	Kilometre(s)
KVIC	-	Khadi and Village Industries Commission
KWT	-	Kuruskal-Wallis Test
LAMPS	-	Large-Size Adivasi Multi Purpose Societies
LBS	-	Lead Bank Scheme
LDBs	-	Land Development Banks
LGR	-	Linear Growth Rate
LIBOR	-	London Inter-Bank Offer Rate
loc. cit.	-	Loco citats (in the place cited)

LPG	-	Liberalisation, Privatisation and Globalisation
LQ	-	Locational Quotient
MFA	-	Modified Factor Analysis
NABARD	-	National Bank for Agriculture and Rural Development
NBC	-	Net Bank Credit
NCC	-	National Credit Council
NBFCs	-	Non-Banking Financial Companies
No.(s)	-	Number(s)
NPAs	-	Non-Performing Assets
NPBs	-	New Private Sector Banks
NPLs	-	Non-Performing Loans
OLS	-	Ordinary Least Square
op. cit.	-	opere citato (in the work cited)
OSCBs	-	Other Scheduled Commercial Banks
OUP	-	Oxford University Press
p.	-	page
PACS	-	Primary Agriculture Credit Societies
PCA	-	Principal Components Analysis
PEP	-	Productivity, Efficiency and Profitability
PLDBs	-	Primary Land Development Banks
PLR	-	Prime Lending Rate
Pop.	-	Population
pp.	-	pages
PSBs	-	Public Sector Banks
PSCs	-	Primary Service Co-operatives
Pub.	-	Public
Pvt.	-	Private
Q.H.	-	Quarterly Handout

R	-	Rural
RBI	-	Reserve Bank of India
RE	-	Resource Efficiency
RRBs	-	Regional Rural Banks
SAA	-	Service Area Approach
SBI	-	State Bank of India
SCBs	-	Scheduled Commercial Banks
SD	-	Standard Deviation
SFI	-	Specialised Financial Institution
SIDBI	-	Small Industrial Development Bank of India
SLR	-	Statutory Liquidity Ratio
Sq.	-	Square
S-U	-	Semi-Urban
UCBs	-	Urban Co-operative Banks
viz.	-	videlicet (namely)
Vol(s)	-	Volume(s)
WCI	-	Weighted Composite Index
ZST	-	Z-Sum Technique

CONTENTS

1

INTRODUCTION

Infrastructure plays a crucial role in the development of an economy. In infrastructure, financial sector occupies a prominent place, as it provides the very essential finance, which lubricates well the wheels of the vehicle of development. The role of financial sector in the process of economic development has been well recognized by the distinguished economists like Schumpeter, Kalecki, Keynes, Gurley and Shaw. Among the financial entities, commercial banks are the predominant financial intermediaries. In fact, financial intermediation in India has largely been synonymous with banking.

Commercial banks are the kingpin of all economic activities. The growing importance of these banks is reflected in business, agriculture and industries in India. These banks are most important in terms of their strength and sweep among the financial institutions. It is well recognized that the commercial banks are instrumental in shaping the economic destiny of a country[1]. They are considered as the nerve centres of economics and finance of a nation and the barometers of its economic prospective.[2]

Every country, whether developed or developing, has economically advanced and backward regions. The co-existence of economically developed and relatively depressed states and regions in a country is known as regional inequality or regional imbalance. The problem of regional imbalances has become more serious and grave in developing countries like India. Economic disparities have become the impediments in the path of economic development in India. The main objective of economic development is to reduce inter-personal disparities. But, this target can not be achieved unless inter-regional disparities are reduced to the desired level.

In fact, inspite of more than fifty-five years of economic planning, the pattern of regional development of Indian economy is far from being balanced one. Here, a few states are relatively more developed and many others are economically backward. It is only through balanced regional development that the benefits of economic growth can reach to all the persons living in different states and regions of the country.

The balanced development of an economy implies harmonious development of all the states and regions. But, it does not imply that the rate of development of all regions should be equal and uniform. It simply means that the difference in economic development of different regions should be minimized and reduced to the lowest possible level.

The role of commercial banks in achieving balanced regional development can hardly be over emphasized. They help in this direction by suitably designing their policies in favour of backward and unbanked areas. By opening their branches in backward areas, banks make credit facilities available to the disadvantage sectors. Also, the funds collected from developed regions, may be channelised for investment in underdeveloped regions of the country. In this way, they bring about more balanced regional development.

The economic and commercial activities of commercial banks exert a significant importance on the size and composition of aggregate economic variables--national income, output, employment, consumption, saving and investment etc. Since the banks have stupendous investment potential, they can make a significant contribution in eradicating poverty and unemployment and can bring about a progressive reduction in inter-regional/ state, inter-sectoral and inter-personal disparities.

Role of Commercial Banks in Economic Development

Commercial banks play an important role in the development

of a country. A sound, progressive and dynamic banking system is a fundamental requirement for economic development.[3] A well developed banking system is a necessary pre-condition for economic development in a modern economy.Besides providing financial resources for the growth of industrialization, banks can also influence the direction in which these resources are to be utilized.

As an important segment of the tertiary sector of an economy commercial banks act as the backbone of economic growth and prosperity by acting as a catalyst in the process of development.[4] They inculcate the habit of saving and mobilise funds from numerous small households and business firms spread over a wide geographical area. The funds so mobilized are used for productive purposes in agriculture, industry and trade.[5] In modern economy, banks are considered not merely as dealers in money, but also the leaders in development. They are not only the storehouses of the country's wealth, but also the reservoirs of resources necessary for economic development. It is the growth of commercial banking that facilitated the occurrence of industrial revolution in Europe during the 18th and 19th centuries. Similarly, the economic progress in the present day developing economies largely depends upon the growth of sound banking system in these economies. Commercial banks can contribute to a country's economic development in a number of ways.

A developing economy faces many problems like poverty, scarcity of capital, lack of entrepreneurship etc. There is dependence on agriculture and at the same time agriculture is not modernized. Means of transport are underdeveloped.[6] There are inter-regional and inter-sectoral disparities. There is unequal distribution of wealth. Banks can work catalytic agents of growth by following the right kind of policies in their working, depending upon the socio-economic conditions prevailing in a country.[7] The commercial banks render vital services to the masses belonging to the various sectors of the economy like agriculture, industry whether small scale or large scale, and to the tertiary sector.[8]

As a type of business, commercial banks are middlemen between depositors and borrowers.[9] They play a significant role through their function of financial mediation. They mobilise the resources of those who have excess of them and due to some reasons can not make more profitable and productive use of them and lend these resources to those who have additional opportunities of investment due to entrepreneurial abilities. They in this way guide the flow of resources in most productive channels.[10] Apart from this, the commercial banks help the economic development of a country by faithfully following the monetary policy of the central bank. In fact the central bank depends upon the commercial banks for the success of its monetary policy formulated keeping in view the requirements of a developing economy.[11] Commercial banks also perform a number of other allied functions, such as providing remittance facilities inland as well as foreign to their customers, undertaking agency functions, buying and selling securities, collecting dividend and interest and acting as underwriters of security issues.[12]

The commercial banks help the development of the industrial sector by providing finance to it in many ways. They provide short term, medium term, and long term loans to industry.[13] In India commercial banks grant loans to small scale industrial units for expansion, modernization and renovation and also provide them with working capital finance. Besides industrial units, loans are also granted to technocrats, technologists, technicians and entrepreneurs to set-up small scale industrial units. Banks also give finance for promotion of industrial estates for purchase of land and construction of sheds.[14]

The need of banking institutions is felt rather deeply in the under developed economies in the sense that these economies are usually capital deficient and the task of mobilization of resources and their channelisation to the priority sectors belongs to such institutions.[15] Among the factors determining economic growth in under developed countries capital is of supreme importance.[16] It is regarded not only as central to the process of development but also as strategic.[17] The poorer a country is, in fact, the greater is the need for agencies to collect and invest savings of the masses and invest them in the most productive purposes.[18]

An increasing rate of saving is essential for the increasing requirements of capital formation for a developing country. The savings can be put to direct productive use or can be invested in bank deposits, Govt. securities, equitics, bonds etc. The scope for direct productive use of voluntary savings is however limited in a developing economy in which there exists a very large number of persons whose saving potential is low, because their incomes are very low and financial institutions are inadequate. Further, rural people who belong to high income group, their saving potential is high; such income earners tend to hold their savings mainly in currency, and to some extent in jewelry, in land or in the form of loans and advances given to unorganized markets, i.e. in forms which are socially wasteful. Often they do so because of such factors as their ignorance of the availability of different types of financial assets in which they can hold their savings.[19] The commercial banks in these situations can help in mobilization of savings, through branch expansion in unbanked and underbanked areas and by introducing a variety of deposit schemes to suit the needs of individual depositors. Thus, they can help in accelerating the rate of capital formation in a developing economy.[20]

All the underdeveloped countries have primarily agricultural economies, with low level of income, low standard of living and high propensity to consume. Low level of income and high propensity to consume leads to low capital formation. These economies, therefore, suffer from vicious circle of poverty. Moreover, with the existence of large non-monitised sector in the economy and the prevalence of widespread illiteracy and conservatism among the masses, savings remain either unutilized or hoarded in the form of cash, gold and silver. Thus, the savers' peculiar preferences are also responsible, with other factors for the meager capital formation.[21] Therefore, any effort to develop the economy requires an action to increase, mobilize and appropriately channelise the domestic financial resources towards productive investment in the economy. This calls for not merely the presence but also an active role of banking and other financial institutions to meet the emerging needs of the economy.[22]

The commercial banks help the large agricultural sector in a number of ways. They open a network of branches in rural areas to provide agricultural credit. They provide finance directly to agriculturists for the marketing of their produce, for the modernization and mechanisation of farms, for providing irrigation facilities, for developing land, etc. They also provide financial assistance for animal husbandry, dairy farming, sheep breeding, poultry farming and horticulture.[23] The small and marginal farmers, landless agricultural workers, artisans and petty shopkeepers in rural areas are provided finance through regional rural banks (RRBs). These RRBs operate under a commercial bank. Thus the commercial banks meet the credit requirement of all types of rural people.[24]

The commercial banks advance credit for the development of employment generating activities in developing countries. They provide loans for the education of young persons studying in engineering, medical and other vocational institutions of higher learning. They advance loans to young entrepreneurs, medical and engineering graduates and other technically trained persons in establishing their own business. Such loan facilities are provided by a number of commercial banks in India. Thus, the banks not only help in human capital formation but also in increasing entrepreneurial activities in developing countries.[25] In the industrial field banks serve as friend, philosopher and guide to industrial units. They provide short term, medium term and long term credit to industries for their establishment, expansion, modernization and renovation. But, their role is not limited only to provide finance to the industries, rather they play an important role in the revival of sick units. They nurse a large number of sick units with a view to enable them to continue their production and maintain their level of employment. Banks set up cells, manned by expert, technical personnel to advise industrial units, as how to recognize their production plan and make arrangements for better financial management and cash flows.[26]

Modern Indian commercial banks have diversified their activities with their entry into new non traditional areas of business. These new areas include mutual fund, merchant banking activities, management of capital issues, portfolio management, corporate counseling, project counseling, underwriting of capital issues, hire-purchase finance, equipment leasing, venture capital and factoring services.[27] In fact, the whole history of the development of banking system in India since independence, particularly after the bank nationalization in 1969, is a story of numerous diversifications and innovations introduced in the functioning of banks with a view to expand and improve their performance in accordance with the changing needs of the economy. These new activities by banks and their subsidiaries result in the development of industry and trade in the country.[28]

Recent times have witnessed drastic transformations in the style of banking. Developing countries need large bank funds to finance foreign trade. Developing economies, despite aid from developed countries have been persistently subjected to an adverse balance of trade. In this context, commercial banks help the developing countries in their process of import substitution and export promotion.[29] The commercial banks help in developing both the internal and external trade of a country. They provide loans to retailers and wholesaler for their inventory. They also help in the movement of goods from one place to another by providing facilities like discounting and accepting bills of exchange, providing overdraft facilities and issuing drafts etc. Moreover, they finance both exports and imports of developing countries by providing foreign exchange facilities to importers and exporters of goods.[30]

The role of commercial banks in establishing an egalitarian society is also important. They can help in this direction by suitably amending their lending policies. Commercial banks' too much insistence on the safety of their advances will motivate them, to lend to the people who can furnish good security.[31] In these circumstances, people of low means are not in a position to avail them the facility of credit. Thus, the commercial banks can design their lending policies in such a way as to ensure sufficient credit to the neglected sectors of the economy and to those who do not have easy access to credit. Hence, the commercial banks can bring down the inter-regional, inter-sectoral and inter-personal disparities.

In terms of their role in a planned economy, the commercial banks may be distinguished from other financial institutions in as much as the former assist in the implementation of government plans by providing the sinews of development. This role has assumed an added significance for India's development efforts through successive five year plans.[32]

Broadly speaking, the commercial banks have been assigned the task of accelerating the economic growth by bringing about a revolution in different sectors of the economy and better distribution of income and wealth, reducing unemployment and inter/intra-regional economic disparities and ameliorating the economic lot of the vast majority of people living in substandard economic conditions.[33]

To sum up, banks have become an omnibus institution in the modern times to which people of varied interests look for help and success. The services rendered by a modern commercial bank is of inestimable value. It mobilizes the scattered savings of the community and redistributes them into more useful channels. It enables large payments to be made over long distances with maximum safety and minimum expenses. It constitutes the very life blood of economic society.[34]

History of Banking in India

Banking in India is of ancient origin. It flourished here even during the early vedic period. However, the commercial banking in India began in 1770 with the establishment of the first joint stock bank, named 'The Bank of Hindustan' by an English Agency (Alexander & Company) in Calcutta. Around 1784, the Bengal Bank was set up and thereafter in 1786, the General Bank of India was established. But, sooner or later all these banks failed due to one or other reason.

In fact, real beginning of the modern commercial banking in the country was made with the establishment of the 'Bank of Bengal' in 1806. Later on, 'The Bank of Bombay' and 'The Bank of Madras' were set up in 1840 and 1843 respectively. These three banks were called the Presidency Banks. They were partly financed by East India Company and were given the right to issue paper currency notes in their own regions, till 1862.

In 1881, the first purely Indian bank i.e Oudh Commercial Bank came into being. It was followed by the setting up of the Punjab National Bank in 1894 and the People's Bank in 1901. The Swadeshi Movement of 1905 encouraged the growth of commercial banks in India. The major banking events during the inter-war period(1918-39), were the amalgamation of the three Presidency

Banks into the Imperial Bank of India in 1921 and the setting up of the Reserve Bank of India in 1935. After the establishment of Reserve Bank of India, the Imperial Bank ceased to act as the Government Banker and Banks' Banker. It was, however decided, that Imperial Bank of India will function as the sole agent of RBI at all places in India where the latter had no branches.[35] Then came the period of banking crisis. During 1913-48 about 1100 banks failed. Thus, pre independence history of Indian commercial banking is marked by checked growth. It has long periods of slow growth intervened by short periods of rapid growth, but followed by great banking crisis.

When India became independent in 1947, it inherited an extremely weak banking structure, with 640 banks of which only 96 were scheduled banks and the rest small non-scheduled banks. The banking facilities were heavily concentrated in metropolitan centers, cities and port towns, with a very high proportion of total advances going to trade. [36]

Commercial banking has changed substantially after the independence due to nationalization and tighter government control and supervision over banking operations. On July 1, 1955, The Imperial Bank of India was nationalized and renamed as State Bank of India (SBI). Subsequently, in 1960 eight more banks, which had been operating in erstwhile princely states of India, were converted into the subsidiaries of SBI. From the beginning of 1963, the number of subsidiaries of SBI, was reduced to seven[37], as the two subsidiaries namely, State Bank of Bikaner and State Bank of Jaipur were merged together to form State Bank of Bikaner and Jaipur.

Subsequently, the scheme of social control over banks came into force on Feb 1, 1969. The main objectives of the scheme were, to achieve a widespread of bank credit, preventing its misuse, directing a large volume of credit to flow into the neglected sectors and making it an increasingly effective instrument of economic development.[38]

However, the scheme of social control over banks failed largely to achieve its objectives, as it was difficult to achieve them under the system of private ownership of banks. Hence, direct control on the functioning of commercial banks was considered essential. As a consequence, fourteen major private sector commercial banks, each having deposits more than Rs. 50 crore, were nationalized on 19th July, 1969.[39] The fundamental change that was intented to be introduced was the rapid transformation of purely profit-oriented private owned and urban biased banking sector into a development oriented and social justice based public sector banking industry. The purpose was to convert the banking of classes into the banking of masses.

Nationalisation, thus, in short, aimed at to accelerate development and thus make a significant impact on the problems of poverty and unemployment and to bring about progressive reduction in disparities between the rich and poor sections of people and between the relatively advanced and backward areas of our country.[40]

In 1975, the Govt. of India appointed a working group under the chairmanship of Shri. M. Narsimhan to review the flow of institutional credit especially to the weaker sections of the community. The group identified certain deficiencies in the role of the two major agencies in the field, the co-operative credit institutions and the commercial banks. It was also concluded that geographical and financial gaps in the rural credit can not be met within a reasonable period by reorganizing or restructuring the two systems. At the same time, it recognized certain commendable features in both systems which could be combined in a new type of institution. Therefore, the working group recommended the setting up of state sponsored, regionally based and rural-oriented banks called Regional Rural Banks (RRBs).[41] In this way, in October 1975, RRBs were set up to develop agriculture, small scale industry, trade and other productive activities in rural areas by providing credit and other facilities, particularly to agriculture labourers, artisans and small entrepreneurs. Presently, there are 196 regional rural banks in India. They are working in all the states of the country, except for Sikkim and Goa.

Afterwards, on April 15, 1980, another six private sector commercial banks, each having deposits worth Rs. 200 crore or more, were nationalized.[42] Thus, with the nationalization of these banks the number of nationalized banks went up to 28 and more than 90 per cent of banking came under public control.[43] But, after the merger of New Bank of India with Punjab National Bank with effect from September 4, 1993, the number of nationalized banks got reduced from 28 to 27.

Undoubtedly, the commercial banks in India have made phenomenal progress after nationalization. The highlights of nationalized banking have been greater stress on district credit planning; revamping of branch expansion policy; intensive hunt for deposits mobilization; introduction of schemes and programmes like Lead Bank Scheme, Differential Rate of Interest Scheme, 20 point Economic programme, Integrated Rural Development Programme (IRDP) and schemes for unemployment graduates etc. Thus, commercial banks adopted a new social philosophy of achieving socialistic pattern of society through allocation of resources to the poor and under-privileged classes, thereby raising levels of employment and income.[44]

Financial Sector Reforms

The year 1991-92 was a watershed in the economic history of India.[45] During this year many reforms were introduced in the Indian banking sector. A framework of these reforms was provided by the report of the *Committee on Financial System,* popularly known as Narasimham Committee-I. These reforms sought to enhance the efficiency, productivity and challenges which a market driven, competitive and outward looking Indian economy would place on the financial system and prepare it for the 21st century.[46] Shri M. Narasimham chaired another committee on banking sector reforms, which tabled its report on April 23, 1998. This committee is also known as the Narasimham Committee-II. On the basis of the recommendations of these committees, a number of banking sector reforms have been introduced for improving the efficiency and to promote competition in the banking sector to enable it to respond more effectively to the emerging needs of the liberalized Indian economy.

The major reforms introduced so far may be broadly classified into four areas.[47] *One,* there are overall monetary policy issues relating to interest rates and exchange rates, reduction in SLR and CRR, modifications in refinance facilities, development of alternative system of monetary controls, development of securities and capital markets, etc. *Two,* the measures for strengthening banks by way of transparency in the financial statements of banks, clearing up of balance sheets by way of prescription of prudential norms for income recognition, asset classification and provisioning for impaired assets, and improving the risk absorption capacity by adopting prudential norms for capital adequacy. Computerisation of banking transaction, recognition of individual institutions to enhance competitive capabilities and facilitate provision of better services to customers, autonomy to public sector bank managements in managing the affairs of individual banks, machinery for customer grievances redressal etc. fall into this category. *Three,* there are steps to enhance competition in the financial sector by allowing entry of private Indian and foreign banks, giving more freedom to expand the operations of existing private banks and widening the scope of activities of banking and non-banking institutions. *Four,* there are issues relating to strengthening the regulation and supervision over banks and more particularly over the very large number of non-banking financial institutions.

The reforms introduced in the banking sector have become a continuous process aimed at improving financial strength and functional efficiency of the commercial banks and bringing them to the international standards. The outcome of the various reform measures so far has been impressive and banks have responded increasingly to competitive environment by restructuring their operations and upgrading performance standards. Introduction of a more transparent balance sheet format, capital adequacy and prudential norms have helped to bring out the true strengths and weaknesses of each bank. These reforms have created strong compulsions for improving the working of banks.[48]

Structure of Banking System in India

The Indian banking system consists of a number of institutions; comprising Reserve Bank of India, Indian Commercial Banks, Co-operative Banks, Regional Rural Banks, Foreign Banks and other specialized banking institutions. The structure and composition of banks in India is given in exhibit 1.

EXHIBIT 1

BANKS IN INDIA

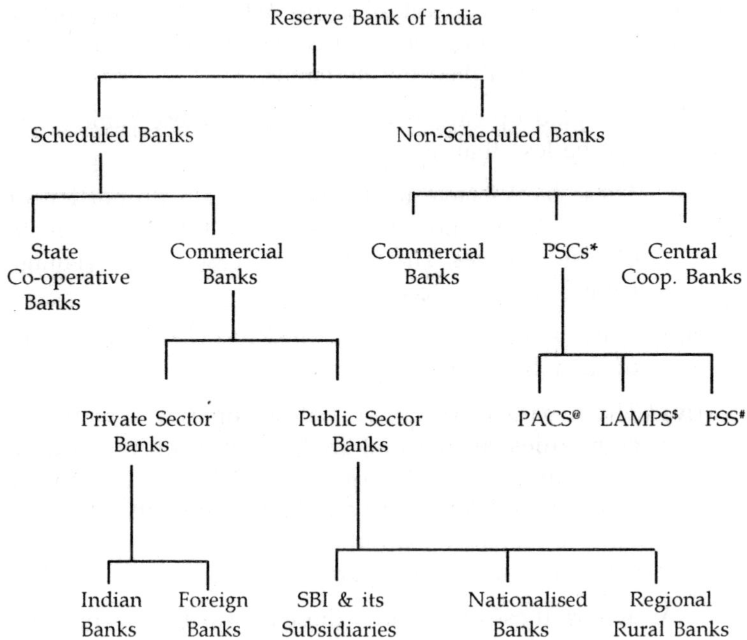

*PSCs : Primary Service Co-operatives

@PACSS : Primary Agricultural Credit Societies

$LAMPS : Large-Sized Adivasi Multipurpose Societies

#FSS : Farmers Service Societies

It is evident from the exhibit that Reserve Bank of India is the apex bank of country. It was established on April 1, 1935 and then nationalized on March 1, 1949. It exercises wide powers of control and supervision over commercial banks under RBI Act, 1934, and Banking Regulation Act, 1949. It gives directions to banks regarding the credit policy to be followed, the margins to be kept and the rate of interest to be charged etc. Thus, as a central banking authority, RBI occupies a pivotal position in the Indian Banking system.

The banks in India are grouped into two categories; schedule and non-schedule banks. The banks included in the second schedule of the Reserve Bank of India Act, 1934 are known as *scheduled banks*. To be eligible for this, the following conditions are required to be fulfilled by the banks:

(i) The paid-up capital and reserves of these banks must not be less than Rs. 5 lacs,

(ii) These banks have to deposit a certain proportion of their demand and time liabilities with RBI in the form of cash reserves. The RBI can increase this percentage from 3 to 15 per cent,

(iii) These banks have to send to the RBI a weekly statement of their financial affairs, and

(iv) These banks are either state-co-operative banks or companies as defined in Section 3 of the Indian Companies Act, 1956 or corporations or companies incorporated by/under any law in force in any place outside India or institutions notified by the Central Government in this regard.[49]

As against these obligations, these banks, in turn enjoy the facility of financial accommodation and remittance facilities at concessional rates from the RBI.

The banks, which are not included in the second schedule, are *non-scheduled banks*. The Reserve Bank of India exercises no special control on these banks, though they have to send to the RBI, monthly statements of their financial affairs. The non-scheduled commercial banks are not eligible for having loans from RBI for carrying out their day-to-day general activities. But, under emergency conditions they can be granted loans by RBI.

The scheduled banks are further divided into two categories; co-operative and commercial banks. *Co-operative banks* play a crucial role in Indian financial system. The co-operative credit system in India mainly consists of (i) the long term agricultural credit institutions, and (ii) the short term agricultural credit institutions.

To provide long term credit to the farmers, there is a two tier system in the co-operative sector in India. It consists of:

(i) Central Land Development Banks at the apex, and

(ii) Primary Land Development Banks at the base level.

Each primary land development bank is affiliated to a central land development bank. In some states, there are no primary land development banks but central land development bank has its branches to lend term credit.[50]

The short term agricultural credit institutions have a three tier structure, consisting of:

(i) State Co-operative Bank - an apex body in a state.

(ii) District/Central Co-operative Banks–intermediaries at the district level, and

(iii) Primary Service Co-operatives (PSCs), which comprise: Primary Agricultural Credit Societies (PACS), Large - Sized Adivasi Multipurpose Societies (LAMPS) and Farmers Service Societies (FSS), at the grassroot(village) level.

Thus, the cooperative credit structure is generally based on a three tier organizational set up. But, in some smaller states and union territories, mainly on account of smaller jurisdictional coverage, there exists a two tier structure, with the State Co-operative Bank at the apex, directly financing primary societies at the base level.[51]

A commercial bank is that bank which mainly lends its funds to the commercial sector of economy, i.e., to traders and merchants. The modern commercial banks, also carry out other ordinary banking business of receiving deposits, advancing loans, discounting bills etc. The terms; commercial banks, joint-stock banks, member banks and credit banks are usually used interchangeably.

All scheduled commercial banks taken together account for more than 99.9 per cent of total business of commercial banks in India. The remaining, less than 0.1 per cent of total business is performed by non-scheduled commercial banks. At the end of March 2004, there were 287 commercial banks in the country, of which 286 were scheduled commercial banks and only one was non-scheduled commercial bank.[52]

Scheduled commercial banks in India are further divided into two categories; Indian and Foreign banks. *Indian banks* are those which have been incorporated in India and so have their head offices in India. *Foreign banks*, on the other hand, have been incorporated in foreign countries and have their head offices outside India. The bulk of banking business in India, is in the hands of Indian banks. But, foreign banks also occupy a place of importance in the field of merchant banking (i.e., underwriting and promotion of new capital issues).[53]

Indian scheduled commercial banks are operating both in private and public sector. The *public sector banks* constitute the dominant part of commercial banking in India. They include; the Regional Rural Banks, State Bank of India and its seven subsidiaries, fourteen banks nationalized in July 1969 and six[54] banks nationalized in April 1980. These public sector banks control more than 75 per cent of the total scheduled commercial banking business in India (Table 1.1).

Commercial banking system in India consisted of 286 scheduled banks and one non-scheduled bank at the end of March 2004. Of the scheduled banks; 33 were foreign banks, 30 private banks (21 old + 9 new) and 223 public sector banks. The public sector banks consisted of 196 Regional Rural Banks (RRBs), 19 nationalised banks, State Bank of India and 7 associates of State Bank of India.[55]

The relative share of different bank groups in total banking business in India, has been exhibited in Table 1.1. It is evident from the table that the public sector banks accounted for more than 91 per cent of the number of branches and nearly 75 per cent of total banking business of all Scheduled Commercial Banks in India. On the other hand, the foreign banks which accounted for a very negligible share (0.3%) in the number of branches succeeded to capture nearly 6 per cent of the total banking business of all Scheduled Commercial Banks in the country.

TABLE 1.1

Bank Group wise Branches, Deposits and Credit of Scheduled Commercial Banks in India. March, 2004

(Amt. in Rs. Lacs)

Bank Group	*No. of Branches*	*Total Deposits*	*Total Credit*
SBI and its subsidiaries	13699 (20)	36089922 (23.9)	20846504 (23.7)
Nationalised Banks	34220 (49.9)	75244110 (49.8)	40810526 (46.4)
Foreign Banks	208 (0.3)	7270491 (4.8)	6361479 (7.2)
Regional Rural Banks	14663 (21.4)	5590902 (3.7)	2602034 (3.0)
Other Scheduled Commercial Banks	5855 (8.5)	26940914 (17.8)	174106.61 (19.8)
Total Scheduled Commercial Banks	68645 (100.0)	151127339 (100.0)	88031203 (100.0)

Source : Compiled from RBI, Banking Statistics(Basic Statistical Returns), Bombay, March 2004.

Notes : Figures in parentheses represent percentage share of the respective bank group in total.

NOTES AND REFERENCES

1. H.L. Sharma, ***Commercial Banking Development***, Rajat Publications, New Delhi 2003, p. 1.

2. B.P. Sharma, ***The Role of Commercial Banks in India's Developing Economy***, S. Chand and Company Ltd., New Delhi 1974, p. 85.

3. K. Padmanabhan, "Lead Banking and District Credit Plan : A Case Study" in V.S. Mahajan(ed.) ***Studies in Indian Banking and Finance***, Deep & Deep Publications, New Dehli, 1989, p. 148.

4. Vasant Desai, ***Indian Banking, Nature and Problems***, Himalaya Publishing House, Bombay, 1979, p. 9.

5. E.W. Reed, ***The Commercial Bank Management***, A Harper international student Reprint, 1964, p. 1.

6. M.L. Jhingan, ***Money Banking and International Trade***, Konark Publications, New Delhi, 1986, p. 252.

7. S. Sing, ***Performance Budgeting for Commercial Banks in India***, The Macmillan Company of India Ltd., New Delhi, 1997, p. 5.

8. A.K. Vashist, ***Public Sector Banks In India***, H.K Publishers and Distributors, New Delhi, 1991, p. 4.

9. Colin D. Campbell and Rosemary Campbell, ***An Introduction to Money and Banking***, The Dryden Press, Hinsdale, Illions, New Hampshire, 1981, p. 126.

10. W.M. Decay, ***The British Banking Mechanism***, London, 1960, p. 16.

11. A.K. Vashist, *op. cit.*, p.8.

12. S. C. Garg, ***Indian Banking Cost and Profitability***, Anmol Publications, New Delhi, 1989, p. 2.

13. Jhingan, *loc. cit.*

14. Report of banking commission, 1972, p. 64.

15. B.S. Bhatia and A.S. Chawla, "Banking and new Economic Programme," in S.D. Tripathi and K.K. Uppal(eds.) ***Banking and New Economic Programme***, Publication Bureau, P.U. Chandigargh, 1984, p. 63.

16. Sharda Prasad, "Role of Banks in a Developing Economy" in P. D. Hajela (ed.), ***Role of Commercial Banking in a Developing Economy***, Popular Prakashan, Bombay, 1969, p. 55.

17. C.P. Kindleberger, Economic Development, McGraw Hill Book Company, INC New York, 1965, p. 83.

18. G.M. Meier, ***Leading Issues in Economic Development : Studies in International Poverty***, (ed. 2) Oxford University, Press, London 1970, pp. 112-13.

19. Report of the Banking Commission 1972, pp. 85-86.

20. M.L. Jhingan, *op. cit.* p. 253.

21. S. N. Ghoshal and M.D. Sharma ***Economic Growth and Commercial Banking in a Developing Economy***, Scientific Book Agency, Calcutta, 1965, p. 6.

22. RBI, ***Banking and Development***, Report of an International Seminar, 1970, p. 1.

23. ***Report of Banking Commission***, 1972, p. 64.

24. H.L. Sharma, op. cit., p. 3.

25. A.K. Vashist, op. cit., p. 7.

26. R.C. Paul, "The Role of Banking in the New Economic Programme", in J.D. Tripathy and K.K. Uppal (eds.), ***The Role of Banking and the New Economic Programme***, Publication Bureau, Punjab University, Chandigarh, 1984, p. 4.

27. For further readings, N. Nagarajan, "Commercial Banks in Non Traditional Areas," in S. S. Hugar(ed.) ***Trends and Challenges to Indian Banking***, Deep & Deep Publications, 1993, pp. 121-75.

28. H.L. Sharma, *op. cit.*, p. 4.

29. Meenakshi Sooden, ***Regional Disparities of Commercial Banking in India***, Kanishka Publishing House, New Delhi, 1992, pp. 23-24.

30. B.P. Aggarwal, ***Commercial Banking in India***, Classical Publishing Company, New Delhi, 1981, p. 208.

31. *Ibid.*, p. 3.

32. S.C. Garg, *op. cit.*, p. 3.

33. R. S. Sayers, ***Modern Banking***, Oxford University Pres, London, 1951.

34. K.C. Shekhar, ***Banking Theory and Practice***, Vikas Publishing House Pvt. Ltd., New Delhi, 1979, p. 9.

35. Farhat Husain, ***Public Sector Commercial Banking in India***, Deep & Deep Publication, New Delhi, 1986, p. 18.

36. Suraj B. Gupta, ***Monetary Economics***, S. Chand and Company Ltd., New Delhi, 2001, p. 98.

37. Seven subsidiaries of SBI are; State Bank of Bikaner and Jaipur, State Bank of Hyderabad, State Bank of Indore, State Bank of Mysore, State Bank of Patiala, State Bank of Saurashatra and State Bank of Travancore.

38. Govt. of India, ***Report of Banking Commission***, New Delhi, 1972, p. 39

39. Fourteen banks nationalized on July 19, 1969, were; Allahabad Bank, Bank of Baroda, Bank of India, Bank of Maharashtra, Canara Bank, Central Bank of India, Dena Bank, Indian Bank, Indian Overseas Bank, Punjab National Bank, Syndicate Bank, Union Bank of India, United Bank of India and United Commercial Bank.

40. The text of statement made by Prime Minister in Parliament, *The Banker,* July 1969, p. 366.
41. Report of CRAFICARD, Reserve Bank of India, 1981, p. 106.
42. Six banks nationalized on April 15, 1980, were; Andhra Bank, Corporation Bank, New Bank of India, Oriental Bank of Commerce, Punjab & Sind Bank and Vijaya Bank.
43. A.S. Chawla, ***Nationalisation and growth of Indian Banking,*** Deep & Deep Publications, New Delhi, 1987, p. 37.
44. *Ibid.,* p. 19.
45. S.S. Tarapore, "An Assessment of Indian Economic Reforms" ***Prajnan,*** Vol. XXV, No. 3-4, October 1996-March 1997, p. 239.
46. M. Narasimham, "Banking Sector Reforms : The CSF Report and after", ***Prajnan,*** Vol. XXV, No. 3-4, October 1996-March 1997, p. 221.
47. N.P. Kurup, "Banking Sector Reforms and Transparency", ***Economic and Political Weekly,*** Vol. XXXI, No. 12, March 23, 1996.
48. Ishwar. C. Dhingra, ***The Indian Economy Environment and Policy,*** Sultan Chand and Sons, New Delhi, 202, p. 648.
49. M.L. Chhipa, ***Commercial Banking Development in India,*** Printwell Publishers, Jaipur, 1987, p. 42.
50. Ajit Singh, ***Rural Development and Banking in India,*** Deep & Deep Publications, New Delhi, 1985, p. 57.
51. Bhupal Singh Negi, ***Co-operative Credit and Regional Development,*** Deep & Deep Publications, New Delhi, 1990, p. 236.
52. RBI, ***Report on Trend and Progress on Banking in India,*** 2004-05
53. Suraj B. Gupta, *op. cit.,* p. 84.
54. The number of these banks now have come down to five, after the merger of New Bank of India with Punjab National Bank, w.e.f. September 4, 1993.
55. Economic and Political Weekly Vol. XL, No. 12, March 14-25, 2005, p. 1290.

2

REVIEW OF LITERATURE

There is no dearth of research studies conducted on various aspects of commercial banking in India. Whereas, some of the studies are solely concerned with analyzing the inter-regional and inter-state disparities in the expansion of banking activities during the pre and post banking sectors reform period. Others also make an attempt to identify the factors responsible for the regional variations in banking development. Some of the important studies relating to the regional disparities in the commercial banking development in India have been reviewed in the present chapter.

Das et. al,[1] **(2005)** analysed the different efficiency scores of Indian banks (PSBs, Pvts and FBs) for the period 1997-2003, using data envelopment analysis (DEA). The study revealed that the Indian banks were still not much different in terms of input and output oriented technical efficiency and cost efficiency. However, there was much difference with respect to their revenue and profit efficiency. Some of the factors which were found to have a positive impact on average profit efficiency were bank size, ownership structure and being listed on the stock-exchange. Finally, the median efficiency score of Indian banks in general, and of bigger banks in particular were observed to be showing an improvement during the post-reform period.

One more study to examine the efficiency of scheduled commercial banks operating in India during the period from 1986 to 2003, was carried out by **Sarma**[2] **(2005)**. The researcher employed the technique of Stochastic Frontier Analysis (SFA) to estimate bank-specific cost and profit efficiency. The study showed that the cost efficiency of the banking industry witnessed an increase during the period under context. On the contrary, the profit efficiency underwent a decline during the same period. Among different bank groups, the domestic banks appeared to be more efficient than the foreign banks.

Sharma[3] (2005) carried out an analysis to assess the growth of commercial banks in different population groups, during the pre and post financial sector reform period in India. The study pointed out that whereas, the banking sector reforms have been successful in improving the health and efficiency of banking industry in India, they have failed grossly in achieving the objective of growth with equity.

Mohan and Ray[4] (2004) also attempted to make a comparison of the performance of different categories of banks, using their physical quantities of inputs and outputs. For the purpose of computations, panel data for 58 banks, which included 27 PSBs, 20 old private sector banks and 11 foreign banks was analysed for the period 1992-2002. The researchers also compared revenue maximization efficiency of these three groups of banks. The analysis showed that public sector banks performed significantly better than private sector banks. But there was not much difference between the efficiency of PSBs and foreign banks. The better performance of public sector banks was ascribed to higher technical efficiency rather then higher allocative efficiency.

Mallya[5] (2003) carried out an empirical study to ascertain the extent to which the Branch Performance Management System in commercial banks portray the characteristics of well-designed and effective performance management system. For the analysis, a sample of 25 Indian commercial banks, which included 17 public sector banks (PSBs), 6 new private sector banks (NPBs) and two old private sector banks (OPBs) was taken. The data shown in the internal inspection reports of the banks as on March 31, 2001 was analysed by taking into account the parameters like total deposits, total advances profitability, customer services, NPAs and their recovery. The study brought into light that banks attach the greatest importance (close to 40 per cent) to adherence to rules and procedural formality associated with various banking transactions and practices. Deposits and profitability followed by NPA status and recovery management emerged to be at the next order of importance in all the banks. The NPBs as compare to PSBs stood at a better position with respect to the customer service parameter.

Sharma[6] (2003) examined the population group wise growth of scheduled commercial banks in different districts of Himachal Pradesh during 1975-1994, with the help of indicators based on branch expansion, deposit mobilization and credit deployment. In order to measure the growth of banking with respect to the selected indicators linear growth rates were calculated. The inter district disparities were measured with the help of coefficient of variation (C.V) and Herfindahl Index (H.I). Further, in order to find out the level of banking development and extent of variations with respect to all the indicators taken together, the composite indices were constructed with the help of principal component analysis. The study pointed out that during the reference period, Himachal Pradesh not only witnessed a remarkable growth in commercial banking, but also registered a credible fall in inter-district disparities. But, in spite of all that, the state continued to lag far behind the national average with respect to the value of most of the indicators.

Another study to analyse the growth scheduled commercial bank in Himachal Pradesh was conducted by **Sharma and Soodan[7] (2000)**. The analysis was carried out at three points of time i.e for the year 1980, 1990 and 1998. The coefficient of variation (C.V) and Herfindahl Index (H.I) were employed to ascertain the extent of inter-district variation in the spread of banking activities. Further, the composite scores were also obtained by assigning appropriate weights to different indicators with the help of Principal Components Analysis. The study indicated that the inter-district variations with respect to all the banking indicator narrowed down in 1998 as compared to 1980. But, the pace of growth of banking activities in the State decelerated during 1990s as compare to 1980s.

Sarker and Das[8] (1997) made an attempt to examine the inter-bank performance differences in the efficiency of banking sector with respect to profitability, productivity and financial management. The analysis was carried out for the year 1994-95 by using Principal Components Analysis (PCA). The area specific index was worked out for each of the performance criteria, based on fifteen selected indicators. The study showed that there was a wide variation in efficiency among the banks according to their ownership pattern. The performance of public sector banks was found to be relatively poor as compared to the other groups.

Another study analyzing the growth of banking in a particular state was carried out by **Ambiga Devi[9] (1996).** She measured the inter district disparities and the level of banking development in Tamil Nadu during the years 1990 and 1991. Ten indicators relating to different banking aspects were used to capture the level of banking development. Then, the coefficient of variation and weighted composite index (constructed with the help of PCA) were used to find out the extent of variations. The analysis pointed out very wide inter-district variations with respect to branch expansion, priority sector lendings and per-capita advances in the state.

A comparative study to analyse the performance of regional rural banks (RRBs) and other scheduled commercial banks (OSCBs) was conducted by **Sharma[10] (1996)** in Himachal Pradesh. The analysis was carried out at two points of time i.e. for the year 1986 and 1993. The growth of the two bank groups was measured with the help of annual compound growth rates based on different banking indicators. The study revealed that regional rural banks (RRBs) in Himachal Pradesh registered a higher growth rate than the commercial banks with respect to almost all the indicators. But, they (RRBs) continued to be far behind the latter (C.Bs) in terms of the absolute values of the most of the banking indicators.

Sharma[11] (1993) also attempted to measure the growth of commercial banks with respect to branch expansion, deposit mobilization, credit deployment and disbursal of priority sector lendings in Himachal Pradesh during the period the period 1996-1992. In order to analyse the growth of banks with respect to the selected indicators, annual compound growth rates were calculated. The study brought into light that the state witnessed a higher growth rate as compare to the country as a whole with respect to all the banking indicators. But despite that, it lagged far behind the country with respect to the absolute values of most of the indicators.

Sooden[12] (1992) made an attempt to ascertain the extent of inter-state variations in the spread of commercial banking in India, during 1975-87. The coefficient of variation, Herfindahl index, Z sum technique and Principal Components Analysis etc., were used to reach the final results. The researcher concluded that though disparities with respect to most of the indicators narrowed down yet, the relative position of different states did not change much during the reference period. On the basis of the composite index of banking development; Punjab, West Bengal, Maharashtra, Tamil Nadu and Karnataka emerged as highly banked states of India in 1987. On the other hand, Assam, Manipur, Tripura, Bihar, Madhya Pradesh, Uttar Pradesh and Meghalaya emerged as very low-banked states during the same year.

Murthy and Haresh[13] (1991) studied the saving behaviour of the people in the form of deposits and linked it with the level of income and financial intermediation. The researchers also examined the inter-regional disparities in saving and attempted to explain the reasons for the disparities with the help of analysis of variance(ANOVA) technique. The state-wise data for six regions was analysed for the years 1979 and 1989. The study revealed that the states/regions with higher level of income and intense spread of branches had higher level of deposits and vice-versa.

One more study to analyse the variations in the disbursal of bank credit among various regions, states and population groups in India was carried by **Srivastava et. al.[14] (1990)**. They constructed the disparity index to know the extent of variations during 1980-85. The analysis revealed that the inter-state disparities with respect to almost all the indicators narrowed down in 1985 as compared to the year 1980.

Dadibhavi[15] (1988) provided an insight into the trends in disparities in the financial infrastructure development in India during 1971-72 to 1986-87. He constructed a composite index of financial infracture development with the help of Principle Components Analysis(PCA), based on different indicators of branch expansion, deposit mobilization and credit deployment by commercial and co-operative banks. The study indicated that regional disparities in the expansion of financial infracture in the country, narrowed down at a lower rate during eighties as compared to the early post-nationalisation period. Further, Assam, Bihar, Himachal Pradesh and Uttar Pradesh were identified as most backward states in the country in terms of financial infracture development.

Vaish and Chhipa[16] **(1988)** also attempted to measure the regional variations in the development of commercial banking in India, during 1960-61, 1970-71 and 1980-81. They also explained the major factors responsible for these variations. The level of commercial banking development was explained in terms of composite indices, constructed with the help of Modified Factor Analysis (MFA). The regional disparities were measured with the help of coefficient of variation. The impact of various factors on banking development was estimated with the help of multiple regression analysis. The results of the study indicated that per-capita state domestic product, urbanization, banking habits and non commercial banking development etc., were the major factors influencing the level of banking development. On the basis of the study; Punjab, Maharashtra, Kerala and West Bengal emerged as highly banked and Tripura and Orissa as very low developed states of India.

Another well known study was conducted by **Bal Krishan**[17] **(1987)**. He used the Z-sum technique and Herfindahal Index(H.I) to evaluate the performance of Scheduled Commercial Banks in reducing the regional disparities in rural India, during 1975-85. The analysis revealed that though the rural disparities with respect to branch expansion, deposit mobilization and deployment credit came down during the reference period. Yet, there existed a high degree of concentration with respect to per capita deposits and credit.

The inter-state disparities in the development of banking in India were also analysed by **Kannan**[18] **(1987)**. A composite index of banking development based on three indicators, namely; population served per branch, per capita deposits and per capita credit, was constructed with the help of factor analysis(FA) technique for the period 1969-84. The study indicated a substantial reduction in inter-state and regional disparities with respect to the growth of overall banking in the country. However, the degree of concentration was found to be higher in case of credit deployment than in deposit mobilization.

Chippa[19] **(1986)** also studied the pattern of rural banking development and identified the factors affecting it in India, during 1972-79. Seven indicators of the spread of rural banking in eighteen major states of India were taken into account. Further, the technique of Modified Factor Analysis(MFA) was used to construct the composite indices of rural banking development. The analysis showed that the commercial banking system in India had been successful in reducing the inter-state disparities in rural banking development. Further, agricultural and infrastructural development were found to be the main factors influencing the rural banking in the country.

Kondle[20] **(1984)** assessed the achievements of commercial banks in reducing the inter-district variations under the lead bank scheme in Himachal Pradesh. He carried out the analysis with the help of Location Quotient (LQ) method, and concluded that the lead bank scheme had been instrumental in reducing the inter-district disparities in the growth of banking in Himachal Pradesh. On the basis of analysis, the commercial banks exhibited wider inter-district variation than the regional rural and co-operative banks in the spread of branch network in the state. The researcher suggested that increase in rural branches, launching of suitable programmes in accordance with the resource potential of various areas and the supply of adequate technical expertise etc., would prove to be helpful in achieving the goals underlying the lead bank scheme.

The extent of concentration of priority sector and agricultural advances in some selected states of India was analysed by **Angadi**[21] **(1983)**. The analysis was carried out with the help of Ordinary Least Square(OLS) method. The findings revealed that the degree of concentration in both the priority sector and agricultural advances among different states reduced in 1979 as compared to 1969. The growth of co-operative societies and increase in awareness among the people, were found to be the important reasons for the reduction in concentration.

Panda and Sahu[22] (1983) revealed that the commercial banks in India, during 1969-79 succeeded in reducing the regional disparities with respect to branch expansion. However, these banks failed to reduce the variations with respect to disbursal of credit in the country.

Bilgrami[23] (1982) studied the imbalances in the growth of banking in terms of branch expansion, deposit mobilization, credit deployment and priority sector lendings in India, over a decade since nationalization. He analysed the imbalances with the help of Locational Quotient (LQ) method and the method of Elasticity Coefficient (EC). The study revealed that there had been a substantial growth of banking in the country with respect to all the parameters of banking development. But, the disparities among different states and regions with respect to the selected indicators did not come down satisfactorily over the reference period.

Chhipa and Sagar[24] (1981) identified the factors responsible for the variations in the banking development in eighteen major states of India. The techniques of Modified Factor Analysis (MFA) and regression analysis were used to carry out the analysis. Literacy rate urbanization and infrastructural development emerged to be highly responsible for inter-state disparities in the spread of banking in the country.

Sugayya[25] (1979) evaluated the quantitative and qualitative aspects of the performance of scheduled commercial banks in Andhra Pradesh during 1972-76. The analysis revealed that inspite of a massive branch expansion, deposit mobilization and credit disbursal, the performance of scheduled commercial banks in the state in reducing horizontal and vertical disparities remained unsatisfactory.

Varde[26] (1977) carried out an analysis to study the inter-district and intra-district disparities in the spread of bank branch network in India during 1973-79. Population served per branch(PPB) was calculated to measure the overall banking presence in the country. Further, the Polarisation Index (PI) and the Index of Penetration of Banking Network (IPBN) were also calculated to measure the horizontal and vertical disparities. The analysis unveiled that majority of the districts were not fulfilling a pragmatically acceptable pattern of banking presence in the countryside, during the reference period.

In nutshell, the review of literature brings into light that no serious effort have been made towards a critical study analysing the extent and nature of regional disparities in commercial banking development in India. The focus of attention in most of the studies has been on inter-state analysis for the pre-reform period only. Hence, taking into consideration the limitations of the studies conducted so far, the need for a systematic study analysing the extent of inter-regional and inter-state disparities in commercial banking during pre and post financial sector reform period can be hardly over-emphasised.

REFERENCES

1. Abhiman Das, Ashok Naag and Subhash C. Roy, "Liberisation, Ownership and Efficiency in Indian Banking - A Nonparametric Analysis", ***Economic and Political Weekly***, Vol. XL, No. 12, March 19-25, 2005, pp. 1190-97.

2. Rudra Sen Sarma, "Cost and Profit Efficiency of Indian Banks During 1986-2003 - A Stochastic Frontier Analysis", ***Economic and Political Weekly***, Vol. XL, No. 12, March 19-25, 2005, pp. 1198-1208.

3. H. L. Sharma, "Changing Commercial Banking Scenario in India - An Analysis", Paper presented in UGC Sponsored National Seminar on, "Banking and Insurance Sector Changing Economic Scenario : Challenges and Responses", Organised by D.A.V College Jalandher, on November 21st & 22nd , 2005.

4. T. T. Ram Mohan and S. C. Ray, "Comparing performance of public and private sector banks - A Revenue Maximisation Efficiency Approach", ***Economic and Political Weekly***, Vol. XXXIX, No. 12, March 20-26, 2004, pp. 1271-1276.

5. P. D. Mallya, "Performance Management System in Banks", ***Prajnan***, Vol. XXXII, No. 3, October-December 2003, pp. 243-253.

6. H. L. Sharma, "Need to Boost Banking in Himachal Pradesh", ***Yojana***, Vol. 37, No. 17, Sep. 30, 1993, pp. 25-26.

7. H. L. Sharma and Meenakshi Sooden, "Growth of Commercial Banks in Himachal Pradesh", Paper presented in the National Seminar on, "Development Alternatives for Underdeveloped Areas of India - Social Science Perspective", Organised by Deptt. of Economics, H.P.U, Shimla, during April, 24-25, 2000.

8. P. C. Sarker, "Management of Regional Imbalances in Regional Development of India : Graphical Approach", Reserve Bank of

India Occasional Papers, Vol. 10, No. 1, March 1989, pp. 1-37.

9. P. Ambiga Devi, "Regional Disparities in Banking Development in Tamil Nadu – 1991", ***The Indian Economic Journal***, Vol. 44, No. 2, October-December, 1996, pp. 143-46.

10. H.L. Sharma, "Regional Rural Banks in Himachal Pradesh", ***Kurukshetra***, Vol. XLIV, No. 10, July 1996, pp. 41-44.

11. H.L. Sharma, ***Commercial Banking Development-A Study of Himachal Pradesh***, Rajat Publications, New Delhi, 2003.

12. Meenaksi Soodan, ***Regional Disparities of Commercial Banking in India***, Kanishka Publishing House, New Delhi, 1992.

13. Y. Sree Rama Murthy & G. Haresh, "Regional Variations in Banking Business : A Study Based on ANOVA Technique", ***Prajnan***, Vol. XX, No. 1, January-March 1991 pp. 31-43.

14. T.N. Srivastava, S.T.V. Chari and S. Augustine, "Disparities in Deployment", ***The Economic Times***, April 26, 1990, p. 11.

15. R.V. Dadibhavi, "Regional Variations in Financial Infrastructural Development in India", ***Prajnan***, Vol. XVI, No. 4, October-December 1988, pp. 391-408.

16. M. C. Vaish & M. L. Chhipa, "Factors Affecting Regional Commercial Banking Development in India", ***Prajnan***, Vol. XVI, No. 3, July-September 1988, pp. 279-99.

17. Bal Krishan, "Role of Commercial Banks in Removing Regional Banking Disparities in Rural India", ***Prajnan***, Vol. XVI. No. 2, April-June 1987, pp. 145-51.

18. R. Kannan, "Banking Development of Regional Disparities", ***The Indian Economic Journal***, Vol. 35, No. 2, July-September 1987, pp. 58-76.

19. M. L. Chhipa, "Rural Banking Development Pattern of Scheduled Commercial Banks in India", ***Prajnan***, Vol. XV, No. 1, January-March 1986, pp. 49-64.

20. Ramesh Kondle, "Lead Bank Scheme in Himachal Pradesh – Progress and Perspectives", Ph.D. Thesis(Unpublished), Himachal Pradesh University, Shimla, 1984.

21. V. B. Angadi, "Bank Advances to Priority Sector- An Enquiry into the Causes of Concentration", ***Economic and Political Weekly***, Vol. XVIII, No. 13, March 26, 1983, pp. 503-10.

22. J. Panda & P.K. Sahu, "Changing Pattern in the Growth of Commercial Banking in India", ***The Indian Journal of Commerce***, Vol. 36, No. 137, December 1983, pp. 80-94.

23. S.A.R. Bilgrami, ***Growth of Public Sector Banks - A Regional Growth Analysis***, Deep & Deep Publications, New Delhi, 1982.

24. M.L. Chhipa & Sushma Sagar, "Banking Development in India : A Study in to the causes of Regional Differentials", ***Prajnan***, Vol. X, No. 4, October-December 1981, pp. 371-77.

25. N. Sugayya, "Performance of Scheduled Commercial Banks in Andhra Pradesh : An Evaluation", ***Prajnan***, Vol. VIII, No. 2, April-June 1979, pp. 205-21.

26. S.D. Varde, "On the Dimensions of Disparities in Banks Branch Network", ***Prajnan***, Vol. VI, No. 1, January-March 1977, pp. 25-40.

3

RESEARCH DESIGN

Commercial banks are the heart of our financial system. These banks owe their origin to the development of trade and commerce and later to the development of organized industry. Both, functionally and organizationally commercial banking system in India had a pronounced urban orientation. Bank credit percolated to areas and sectors, which were already developed. Backward areas were neglected and a security oriented approach to credit was in vogue. The main aim of the nationalization of these banks was to influence the credit flow in the interest of the weaker section of society and also to backward areas, so as to induce an element of balance in the economic development of various regions and social groups.

One of the important problems faced by developing countries today is the glaring disparities in the level of economic development and variations in the rates of growth of different regions.[1] Apart from glaring and deteriorating rural-urban disparities, the post banking sector reform period has seen considerable widening of inter-state and inter-regional variations in India. The regional imbalances and lopsided growth are not conducive to the national goal of growth with equity and hence social justice. In fact, the unregulated growth leading to regional disparities results in numerous economic, social and political problems. It is therefore, rightly considered that the reduction in regional disparities is of utmost importance in context of social justice, and accelerated growth of national income output, employment and maintaining national integration and unity.

Need of the Study

The thrust of governments economic policies enunciated during the post-nationalisation period has been to bring about an overall socio-economic development coupled with a balanced regional development of the country.[2] The commercial banks are supposed to play a much larger and more dynamic role in achieving the objective of balanced economic development by providing effective institutional credit support to various productive programmes in the desired direction. With the coming up of many new private sector banks and market oriented policies of the financial sector, the responsibilities of the scheduled commercial banks in reducing regional disparities have increased many fold.

Many research studies have been undertaken in India to know the extent and direction of the regional disparities in commercial banking during the pre reform period. However, there is complete dearth of studies analyzing the extent of regional variations in commercial banking during the recent liberalization phase of India economy. Thus, it is an appropriate time to study that to what extent the objective of balanced development of an important infrastructure like commercial banks have been affected by the new policy of liberalization, privatization and globalization (LPG).

Scope of the Study

The present study aims at analyzing the extent and direction of regional disparities in commercial banking development in 25 states of India during the year 1985, 1990, 1995, 2000 and 2005. The states considered for the study are; Haryana, Himachal Pradesh, Jammu & Kashmir, Punjab, Rajasthan, Assam, Manipur, Arunachal Pradesh, Meghalaya, Mizoram, Nagaland, Tripura, Bihar, Orissa, Sikkim, West Bengal, Madhya Pradesh, Uttar Pradesh, Goa, Gujarat, Maharashtra, Andhra Pradesh, Karnatka, Kerala and Tamil Nadu. Furthermore, these states have been grouped into six regions viz., Northern, North Eastern, Eastern, Central, Western and Southern region. The scope of the study is confined to scheduled commercial banks only. It is because these banks are considered to be a fairly representative sample and their analysis appropriately determines the emerging trends in the whole banking sector of the country. The scheduled commercial banks accounted for more than 99.9 per cent of the total business of all the commercial banks in India, at the end of March 2004.[3]

Source and Type of Data

The study is primarily based on secondary data. The relevant data relating to banks have been collected from the publications of Reserve Bank of India – *Banking Statistics (BSRs), Banking Statistics (Quarterly Handout), Statistical Tables Relating to Banking in India and Report on Trend and Progress of Banking in India.* The non–banking data have been collected from the publications of Govt. of India like, Economic Survey and Census of India.

Objectives of the Study

The focal point of the study is to evaluate the inter-regional/ state disparities of commercial banking in India. It seeks to evaluate the performance of scheduled commercial banks in reducing regional disparities in their activities in 25 states of India during pre and post banking sector reform period. The specific objectives of the study are as follows:

i. to analyse the extent and direction of inter-state disparities in banking activities in India during the reference period;

ii. to examine the impact of financial sector-reforms on banking in India; and

iii. to identify the backward states with respect to banking development in India.

Methodology

The main variables on the basis of which the extent and direction of regional disparities in commercial banking in India have been analysed are – branch expansion, deposit mobilization and credit deployment. However, the relevant data relating to these variables was not comparable owning to wide differences in population and area across different states/ regions. The bigger the states/ regions were likely to have large volume of deposits and credit as compared to the smaller one. Hence, in order to make the data comparable, different indicators of branch expansion, deposit mobilization and credit deployment have been selected to assess the regional imbalances. These indicators are :

I_1 : Population served per bank branch,

I_2 : Branches per 10,000 square kms. of area,

I_3 : Deposits per branch,

I_4 : Per Capita deposits,

I_5 : Deposits per 10,000 square kms. of area,

I_6 : Credit per branch,

I_7 : Per Capita Credit,

I_8 : Credit per 10,000 square kms. of area, and

I_9 : Credit deposit ratio.

The relative progress of commercial banks in different states and regions has been ascertained by calculating compound growth rates. The value of compound growth rates have been calculated as follows :

$$g = \left\{ \left[\frac{Vt}{Vo} \right]^{1/t} - 1 \right\} 100$$

Where ; g = Compound growth rate,

Vt = Value of the variable during the current year,

Vo = Value of the variable during the base year, and

t = time period.

For measuring the magnitude and pattern of regional disparities with respect to a particular indicator, co-efficient of variation (C.V) and Herfindahl Index (H.I) have been used.

The value of coefficient of variation (C.V) has calculated as follows :

$$C.V_{it} = \frac{S_{it}}{X_{it}} 100$$

Where ; $C.V_{it}$ = Coefficient of Variation[4] of ith indicator in year t,

S_{it} = Sample standard deviation[5] of ith indicator in year t, and

X_{it} = Mean value of the ith variable in year t.

The value of H.I has been computed as follows :

$$H.I = \frac{\sum_{j=1}^{n} X_j^2}{\left[\sum_{j=1}^{n} X_j\right]^2}$$

Where ; H.I. = Herfindahl Index[6]

X_j = The value of the indicator in j^{th} state.

These measures give an idea of indicator wise disparities but fail to reveal the overall behaviour of all the indicators taken together. The overall inter-state disparities with respect to all the indicators taken together, have been analysed with the help of composite scores of banking development.

The selected indicators of banking development have different measuring units, so in practice they are not comparable with each other. Moreover, they can not be merged together in order to findout the level of banking development in a particular state. Consequently, it is imparitive to make the indicators unit free to achieve the above said goal. For this, the Z-sum technique has been used. This technique "involves standardization of variables so that each standardized variate has zero mean and one as standard deviation".[7] The standardized score have been calculated as follows :

$$Z_{ijt} = \frac{X_{ijt} - X_{jt}}{S_{it}}$$

Where ; Z_{ijt} = Standardised score of the ith indicator(i=1, 2, 3...9) for the jth state(j=1, 2 , 3...25) in the year t(t=1, 2, 3...5),

X_{ijt} = Value of ith indicator for j^{th} state in the year t,

X_{it} = Arithmatic mean of ith indicator in the year t, and

S_{it} = Standard deviation of ith indicator in the year t.

Except for the first indicator (I_1) i.e. population served per bank branch, a rising trend with respect to rest of other indicators reveals a better performance of commercial banks. Therefore, in order to bring homogeneity in data the standardized scores of the first indicator have been constructed by taking reciprocal values.

Finally, the composite index has been constructed by summing up the Z-scores with respect to different indicators as follows :

$$Y_{jt} = \sum_{i=1}^{n} Z_{ijt} \qquad 1 \leq j \leq 25\ ,\ 1 \leq t \leq 5$$

Where ; Y_{jt} is the value of composite score of the jth state in year t.

A rising trend in the value of Y_{jt} reveals a better performance of the respective state with respect to the banking development.

Ultimately, on the basis of composite scores obtained by different states, they have been classified into four categories, viz. highly-banked, moderately-banked, low-banked and very-low-banked. For this quartiles have been considered as cut off points.[8] Area lying to left side of the first quartile depicts very low-banked category. Area between first quartile and mean value is the low-banked, and the area between mean and third quartile reflects the moderately-banked state. Area to the right side of third quartile shows the highly-banked state.

Plan of the Study

The present study compromises of five chapters. The *first introductory chapter* has been divided into four sections. In the first section role of commercial banks in economic development has been discussed. The second section has been devoted to discuss the history of banking in India. The third section provides a bird's eye view of the financial sector reforms in India. Further, the fourth section has been devoted to exhibit the structure of banking system in India. In the *second chapter*, a brief review of studies conducted earlier has been summarized. The *third chapter*, outlines the research design in the form of Need, Scope, Type and Source of Data, Objectives, Methodology, Plan and Limitations of the Study. The *fourth chapter* has been divided into two sections. In the first section, the extent and direction of inter-state variations in banking development with respect to the selected indicators have been examined. The second section analyses the impact of financial sector reforms on banking in India. Finally, the *last chapter* summarises the findings and conclusions of the study and points out some suggestions also.

Limitations of the Study

Though every sincere effort has been made to make the present study comprehensive and flawless, yet due to some unavoidable reasons, it is prone to various limitations. The major limitations of the study are listed below:

i. The first and foremost limitation of the study is that it does not take into account the rise in general price level. If the indicators of deposit mobilization and deployment credit are deflated to the base year, the conclusions drawn are likely to change to a large extent.

ii. Secondly, there may exist very wide intra-state variations in India. But, these variations have not been taken into consideration in the study, as it concentrates only on the inter-state analysis.

iii. The study concentrates on analysing the banking data in quantitative terms only. The qualitative aspects of progress of banking in India have not been analysed. It would have been made more meaningful by evaluating the emerging trends in such qualitative aspects of banking as customer services, job satisfaction and morale of the bank employees etc.

iv. Another limitation of the study is that it analyses the performance of commercial banks in terms of branch expansion, deposit mobilization and credit deployment, which certainly may be impressive and creditable. But, it does not try to find out that at what cost has this been achieved. And to what extent the Productivity, Efficiency and Profitability(P.E.P) has been affected by this progress.

v. Finally, one more limitation of the study is that no statistical method has been used to identify the factors responsible for a given level of banking development in a particular state/region.

NOTES AND REFERENCES

1. V.S. Angadi and M.G. Chachadi, "What Constitutes A Planing Region", in N. K. Subramanaya(ed.), ***Economic Development and Planning in India***, Deep & Deep Publications, New Delhi, 1988, p. 163.
2. H.L. Sharma, ***Commercial Banking Development***, Rajat Publications, New Delhi, 2003, p. 53.
3. Reserve Bank of India, ***Banking Statistics(BSR)***, Bombay, March 2004, p. 1.
4. $$S_{it} = \left[\frac{X_{ijt} - \overline{X}_{jt}^{\,2}}{n - 1}\right]^{1/2}$$
5. $$X_{jt} = 1/n \sum_{i=1}^{n} X_{ijt}$$
6. Its value is always 1/n H.I 1. The unit value depicts complete concentration and 1/n shows complete dispersion.
7. Bal Krishan, "Role of Commercial Banks in Removing Regional Banking Disparities in Rural India", ***Prajnan***, Vol. XVI, No. 2, 1987, p. 146.
8. Meenakshi Sooden, "Inter-State Disparities of Commercial Banks in India", ***Prajnan***, Vol. XXVI, No. 2, 1997-98, p. 145.

4

ANALYSIS AND INTERPRETATION

The present chapter has been divided into two sections, the first section endeavours to analyse the performance of scheduled commercial banks in India with respect to the indicators based on branch expansion, deposit mobilization and credit deployment. The second section purports to evaluate the impact of financial sector reforms on banking in India.

Inter-State Disparities in Banking Development in India

Branch Expansion in India

The Reserve Bank of India, before the banking sector reforms, enforced slowdown in branch expansion in metropolitan areas. On the other hand, steady increases in rural branches were encouraged on the consideration that the scheduled commercial banks had a role to play in branch banking in the process of institutionalisation of rural savings. Subsequently, during the mid 1990s when banking sector reforms began to be implemented based on the recommendations of the Narasimham Committee (Report-I), the above policy perspective underwent a metamorphic change. After the expiry of the five year branch expansion programme of 1990-95, the subject of opening rural branches was left to the commercial judgement of banks. With effect from 1st April, 1995, they have been allowed to close the non-viable rural branches served by two commercial banks.

In Table 4.1 the growth of commercial bank branches in different states during the period from 1985 to 2005 has been

TABLE 4.1
TOTAL NUMBER OF BANK BRANCHES IN INDIA

(Rs. Lacs.)

STATE/REGION	*1985*	*%age*	*1990*	*%age*	*1995*	*%age*	*2000*	*%age*	*2005*	*%age*	*G.R.(%)*
NORTHERN	*7027*	***13.75***	***7851***	***13.73***	***8444***	*13.56*	***9035***	***13.84***	***9443***	***14.28***	***1.489***
Haryana	1102	2.16	1256	2.2	1365	2.19	1508	2.31	1668	2.52	2.094
Himachal Pradesh	545	1.07	695	1.22	769	1.23	787	1.21	799	1.21	1.931
Jammu & Kashmir	726	1.42	746	1.3	806	1.29	827	1.27	858	1.3	0.839
Punjab	1998	3.91	2131	3.73	2285	3.67	2548	3.9	2710	4.1	1.536
Rajasthan	2656	5.2	3023	5.29	3219	5.17	3365	5.16	3408	5.15	1.254
NORTH EASTERN	***1332***	***2.61***	***1576***	***2.76***	***1933***	***3.1***	***1933***	***2.96***	***1897***	***2.87***	***1.784***
Assam	942	1.84	1137	1.99	1260	2.02	1263	1.94	1235	1.87	1.363
Manipur	62	0.12	68	0.12	88	0.14	88	0.13	78	0.12	1.154
Arunachal Pradesh	-	-	-	-	69	0.11	69	0.11	68	0.1	-0.146
Meghalaya	127	0.25	144	0.25	180	0.29	181	0.28	183	0.28	1.843
Mizoram	-	-	-	-	79	0.13	79	0.12	79	0.12	0

STATE/REGION	*1985*	*%age*	*1990*	*%age*	*1995*	*%age*	*2000*	*%age*	*2005*	*%age*	*G.R.(%)*
Nagaland	65	0.13	69	0.12	72	0.12	70	0.11	72	0.11	0.513
Tripura	136	0.27	158	0.28	185	0.3	183	0.28	182	0.28	1.467
EASTERN	***9154***	***17.93***	***10558***	***18.46***	***11597***	***18.62***	***11896***	***18.23***	***11918***	***18.02***	***1.323***
Bihar	4137	8.1	4599	8.04	4985	8	5078	7.78	5077	7.68	1.029
Orissa	1719	3.36	1944	3.4	2179	3.5	2247	3.44	2267	3.43	1.393
Sikkim	-	-	29	0.05	42	0.07	46	0.07	55	0.08	4.359
West Bengal	3308	6.47	3986	6.97	4391	7.05	4525	6.93	4519	8.83	1.572
CENTRAL	***10963***	***21.45***	***12524***	***21.9***	***13283***	***21.33***	***13625***	***20.88***	***13716***	***20.74***	***1.126***
Madhya Pradesh	3694	7.23	4282	7.49	4491	7.21	4562	6.99	4532	6.85	1.028
Uttar Pradesh	7269	14.22	8242	14.41	8792	14.12	9063	13.89	9184	13.89	1.176
WESTERN	***7948***	***15.55***	***8829***	***15.44***	***9814***	***15.76***	***10489***	***16.07***	***10482***	***15.85***	***1.393***
Goa	-	-	-	-	278	0.45	323	0.49	338	0.51	1.973
Gujarat	3069	6.01	3331	5.82	3585	5.76	3732	5.72	3705	5.6	0.946
Maharashtra	4879	9.55	5498	9.61	5951	9.55	6434	9.86	6439	9.74	1.397

STATE/REGION	1985	%age	1990	%age	1995	%age	2000	%age	2005	%age	G.R.(%)
SOUTHERN	***14670***	***28.71***	***15849***	***27.71***	***17213***	***27.64***	***18290***	***28.02***	***18680***	***28.24***	***1.216***
Andhra Pradesh	4113	8.05	4534	7.93	4918	7.9	5226	8.01	5393	8.15	1.364
Karnataka	3905	7.64	4227	7.39	4523	7.26	4840	7.42	4948	7.48	1.191
Kerala	2720	6.32	2824	4.94	3119	5.01	3318	5.08	3493	5.28	1.258
Tamil Nadu	3932	7.69	4264	7.46	4653	7.47	4906	7.52	4846	7.33	1.051
Total Branches	**51104**	**100**	**57187**	**100**	**62284**	**100**	**65268**	**100**	**66136**	**100**	**1.298**
MEAN	**2433.524**		**2599.409**		**2491.36**		**2610.72**		**2645.44**		**0.418**

Source : Compile from R.B.I. Banking Statistics (Basic Statistical Returns), Bombay, Relevant Volumes.
Note : -- indicates nil.

depicted. It is evident from the table that there were only 51,104 branches of Scheduled Commercial Bank in India in 1985, which increased to 66,136 in the year 2005. Thus, the number of bank branches in India registered an annual growth rate of 1.298 per cent during the reference period. The average number of branches per state also went up from 2434 to 2645 during the period under reference.

Among different regions, the southern region followed by central region accounted for the largest number of branches in all the years. The combined share of these two regions in total number of bank branches in the country, stood nearly 50 per cent throughout the period under study. In contrast to it, the North Eastern region accounted for less than three per cent share in the number of branches during most of the years.

The state-wise analysis throws light upon the fact that Uttar Pradesh followed by Maharastra witnessed the largest number of commercial bank branches in all the year under context. These two states jointly accounted for nearly one fourth number of scheduled commercial bank branches of the country. Besides these two states; Bihar, Madhya Pradesh, Andhra Pradesh, Karnatka and Tamil Nadu also witnessed comparatively a large number of bank branches. The individual share of these states in total number of branches stood more than seven per cent almost in all the years. On the other hand, Goa, Sikkim and all the North-Eastern states(except Assam) witnessed the lowest number of bank branches in the country. The individual share of all these states always stood less than one per cent.

The total number of bank branches went up at the highest rate in Sikkim (4.359%). It was followed by Haryana (2.094%), Goa (1.973%) and Himachal Pradesh (1.931%). On the other hand, the number of total bank branches came down in Arunachal Pradesh. In Mizoram also their number remained constant during 1995-2005. Apart from it, Jammu and Kashmir, Nagaland and Gujarat also witnessed a growth rate of less than one per cent per annum in the total number of scheduled commercial bank branches.

Population Served Per Bank Branch in India

As a result of slowdown of branch expansion, the trend of

decline in population served per bank branch has also been arrested. In fact, population served per branch in India was 14590 in 1985, which went up to 16487 in 2005, witnessing an increase of 0.613 per cent during the period under reference (Table 4.2). The population served per branch in India went up due to high rate of growth of population on the one hand and closure of some branches on the consideration of their viability, in the wake of the banking sector reforms on the other hand.

Among the regions, population served per branch stood the highest in the North-Eastern region throughout the period under reference. On the contrary, in 1985 and 1990 the Northern region and in all other years under study the Southern region witnessed the lowest population served per bank branch. It is further clear from the table that in three regions; North-Eastern, Eastern and Central region, the population served per branch stood higher than the national average, during all the years under context.

The state-wise analysis shows that population served per branch stood the lowest in Himachal Pradesh in 1985 and 1990, but during rest of the years this position was occupied by Goa. Beside these two states; Punjab, Kerala and Karnatka also witnessed low population served per branch. On the other hand, banks served the largest population per branch in Manipur throughout the period under reference(except 2000). In most of the years; Assam, Bihar, Nagaland and Uttar Pradesh also witnessed high population served per branch.

The Table further brings into light that the population served per bank branch came down only in five states, in all other states it went up during the period under study. The fastest rate of decline was witnessed by Sikim (-1.431%) followed by Goa (-0.567%), Kerala (-0.308%), Himachal Pradesh (-0.262%) and Assam (-0.169%). On the contrary, population served per bank branch went up at the highest growth rate in Nagaland (4.605%). It was followed by Mizoram (2.594%), Arunachal Pradesh (2.553%) and Jammu and Kashmir (1.741%).

The inter-state disparities with respect to this indicator widened further during the period under study. The value of co-efficient of variation, which was 31.44 per cent in 1985, though

TABLE 4.2

POPULATION SERVED PER BANK BRANCH IN INDIA

STATE/REGION	*1985*	*1990*	*1995*	*2000*	*2005*	*G.R.(%)*
NORTHERN	***11738***	***11653***	***12175***	***12790***	***13749***	***0.794***
Haryana	13013	12795	13316	13639	13954	**0.35**
Himachal Pradesh	8550	7301	7173	7598	8113	**-0.262**
Jammu & Kashmir	9160	10087	10651	11857	12937	**1.741**
Punjab	9174	9339	9546	9375	9653	**0.255**
Rajasthan	14488	14197	15134	16440	18432	**1.211**
NORTH EASTERN	***21644***	***18751***	***17663***	***19520***	***22013***	***0.085***
Assam	23907	19527	19061	20730	23112	**-0.169**
Manipur	26452	26324	23182	26432	34000	**1.263**
Arunachal Pradesh	-	-	13783	15522	17735	**2.553**
Meghalaya	11654	11979	10950	12409	13989	**0.917**
Mizoram	-	-	9671	11000	12494	**2.594**
Nagaland	13692	16768	20500	27043	33694	**4.605**
Tripura	16838	16943	15800	17186	18593	**0.497**
EASTERN	***17926***	***17299***	***17402***	***18728***	***20646***	***0.709***
Bihar	18475	18388	19072	21108	23802	**1.275**
Orissa	16574	15991	15415	16096	17179	**0.179**
Sikkim	-	13655	10833	11413	11000	**-1.431**

West Bengal	17941	16706	16556	17440	18956	**0.276**
CENTRAL	***16336***	***16019***	***16874***	***18360***	***20356***	***1.106***
Madhya Pradesh	15504	15092	15991	17435	19438	**1.137**
Uttar Pradesh	16757	16500	17325	18826	20809	**1.089**
WESTERN	***13374***	***13328***	***13416***	***13892***	***15384***	***0.703***
Goa			4450	4102	4204	**-0.567**
Gujarat	12261	12166	12497	13285	14810	**0.949**
Maharashtra	14075	14032	14389	14735	16300	**0.737**
SOUTHERN	***12156***	***12176***	***11993***	***12010***	***12515***	***0.146***
Andhra Pradesh	14187	14354	14244	14304	14790	**0.208**
Karnataka	10487	10439	10598	10724	11358	**0.4**
Kerala	10051	10167	9672	9510	9449	**-0.308**
Tamil Nadu	13143	12914	12525	12527	13373	**0.087**
MEAN	***14590***	***14348***	***13693***	***14829***	***16487***	***0.613***
SD	**4587**	**4104**	**4311**	**5364**	**6995**	**2.132**
CV(%)		**31.439**	**28.604**	**31.482**	**36.171**	**42.425**
HI(%)		**5.21**	**4.9**	**4.381**	**4.502**	**4.691**

Sources : **i.** Same as for Table 4.1

ii. Director of Census Operations, *Census of India*, 1981, 1991 and 2001. Population census of India 1981, 1991 and 2001 came down to 28.60 per cent in 1990. But, after the year of 1990, the value of coefficient of variation continuously went up and ultimately reached at the level of 42.43 per cent in the year 2005.

Number of Commercial Bank Branches Per 10,000 Square Kms. of Area in India

The geographical coverage of scheduled commercial banks have been measured with the help of the indicator of branches per 10,000 square kms. of area in India (Table 4.3). The Table reveals that bank branches per 10,000 square kms. of area in India were 188 in the year 1985, which went up to 254 in the year 2005, registering a growth rate of 1.504 per cent per annum.

A region-wise Analysis points out that Southern region stood at the top with respect to this indicator during all the years under context. It was followed by the Northern region in 1985 and 1990. But the Western region which ranked the lowest with respect to bank branches per 10,000 square kms. of area showed a very rapid performance and occupied the second position in all other years under study. Thus the bank branches per 10,000 square kms. of area went up at the highest rate in Western region (7.373%) and at the lowest rate in Central region (1.14%).

It is further evident from Table 4.3 that Kerala followed by Goa stood at the top with respect to bank branches per 10,000 square kms. of area throughout the reference period. Besides this; West Bengal, Tamil Nadu, Punjab and Haryana also stood high with respect to this indicator. On the other hand, Arunachal Pradesh witnessed the lowest number of bank branches per 10,000 square kms. of area. Apart from this; Manipur, Meghalaya, Nagaland and Jammu and Kashmir also ranked very low with respect to this indicator.

The number of bank branches per 10,000 square kms. of area went up at the highest rate in Sikkim (4.381%) followed by Haryana (2.096%), Goa(1.973%) and Kerala (1.96%). On contrary, in two states; namely Arunachal Pradesh and Mizoram the number of branches per 10,000 sq kms. of area showed no change during the period 1985-2005. Nagaland, followed by Jammu & Kashmir and Gujarat also showed a low growth rate of less than one per cent per annum with respect to this indicator.

TABLE 4.3

Number of Bank Branches per 10,000 Square Kms of Area in India

STATE/REGION	*1985*	*1990*	*1995*	*2000*	*2005*	*G.R.(%)*
NORTHERN	***855***	***953***	***1030***	***1122***	***1197***	***1.697***
Haryana	249	284	309	341	377	2.096
Himachal Pradesh	98	125	138	141	144	1.943
Jammu & Kashmir	23	33	35	36	38	0.708
Punjab	397	423	454	506	538	1.531
Rajasthan	78	88	94	98	100	1.25
NORTH EASTERN	**374**	**432**	**544**	**543**	**536**	**1.816**
Assam	120	145	161	161	157	1.353
Manipur	28	30	39	39	35	1.122
Arunachal Pradesh	-	-	8	8	8	0
Meghalaya	57	64	80	81	82	1.835
Mizoram	-	-	37	37	37	0
Nagaland	39	42	43	42	43	0.498
Tripura	130	151	176	175	174	1.468
EASTERN	**721**	**879**	**981**	**1011**	**1025**	**1.775**
Bihar	238	264	287	292	292	1.028
Orissa	110	125	140	144	146	1.426
Sikkim	-	41	59	65	78	4.381
West Bengal	373	449	495	510	509	1.566
CENTRAL	***330***	***377***	***400***	***411***	***414***	***1.14***
Madhya Pradesh	83	97	101	103	102	1.036
Uttar Pradesh	247	280	299	308	312	1.175
WESTERN	316	349	1127	1272	1311	7.373
Goa	-	-	751	873	913	1.973
Gujarat	157	170	183	190	189	0.932
Maharashtra	159	179	193	209	209	1.377
SOUTHERN	**1356**	**1440**	**1694**	**1799**	**1859**	**1.59**
Andhra Pradesh	150	165	179	190	196	1.346
Karnatka	204	220	236	252	258	1.181
Kerala	700	727	921	980	1032	1.96
Tamil Nadu	302	328	358	377	373	1.061
MEAN	188	201	231	246	254	1.516
SD	**157.739**	**168.314**	**201.738**	**215.984**	**227.265**	
CV (%)	**83.904**	**83.733**	**87.332**	**87.798**	**89.474**	
HI (%)	**7.967**	**7.56**	**7.637**	**7.887**	**8.034**	

Source : **i.** Same as for Table 4.1

The inter-state disparities with respect to this indicator, as pointed out by the value of co-efficient of variation and Herfindahl Index, also widened further during the period under study. The values of co-efficient of variation and Herfindahl Index, which were 83.82 per cent and 7.97 per cent respectively in the year 1985, went up to 89.59 per cent and 8.03 per cent in the year 2005.

Thus, the inter-state disparities with respect to population served per bank branch as well as number of bank branches per 10,000 sq kms. of area, went up during the period under context.

Deposit Mobilisation in India

An important feature of banking development during the reform period has been the continuance of the tempo of deposit mobilization in the country, despite the drastic reduction in effective rate of interest on all types of deposits. It is clear from Table 4.4 that the aggregate scheduled commercial bank deposits in India, increased from Rs. 75789 crores in 1985 to Rs 1512064 crores in the year 2005, at an annual compound growth rate of 16.14 per cent. On an average, deposits per state rose from Rs. 3940.90 crores in 1985 to Rs. 81394.63 crores in 2005.

The Table further elaborates that among the regions; Western region accounted for more than 28 per cent of total deposits throughout the period under study. It was followed by the Southern region, the share of which always stood more than 23 per cent of the total deposits. On the other hand, North-Eastern region, as in case of number of branches, with respect to total deposits also accounted for the lowest share (less than 2 per cent) throughout the period under study.

The state-wise analysis brings into light that in total deposits percentage share of Maharastra always remained more than 21 per cent. It was followed by Uttar Pradesh and West Bengal in all the years (except 1985) under reference. The percentage share of Uttar Pradesh and West Bengal always stood more than ten per cent and seven per cent respectively. On the other hand, Himachal Pradesh, Sikkim, Goa and all North-Eastern states (except Assam), registered the lowest amount of deposits of commercial banks. The individual share of all these states stood less than one per cent throughout the period under study.

TABLE 4.4

TOTAL DEPOSITS IN INDIA

(Rs. Lacs.)

STATE/REGION	1985	%age	1990	%age	1995	%age	2000	%age	2005	%age	G.R.(%)
NORTHERN	***959612***	***12.66***	***1944521***	***12.76***	***4235803***	***12.62***	***9444371***	***13.06***	***17590000***	***11.63***	***15.653***
Haryana	155257	**2.05**	343601	**2.25**	747904	**2.23**	1705324	**2.36**	3689200	**2.44**	**17.164**
Himachal Pradesh	54582	**0.72**	119774	**0.79**	274413	**0.82**	622061	**0.86**	1226800	**0.81**	**16.839**
Jammu & Kashmir	83082	**1.1**	153928	**1.01**	363038	**1.08**	861572	**1.19**	1727300	**1.14**	**16.384**
Punjab	449834	**5.94**	866790	**5.69**	1788454	**5.33**	3871531	**5.35**	6614500	**4.37**	**14.386**
Rajasthan	216857	**2.86**	460428	**3.02**	1061994	**3.16**	2383883	**3.3**	4332200	**2.87**	**16.152**
NORTH EASTERN	***129951***	***1.71***	***265882***	***1.74***	***608496***	***1.81***	***1320853***	***1.83***	***2769700***	***1.83***	***16.529***
Assam	96893	**1.28**	189118	**1.24**	395587	**1.18**	844415	**1.17**	1808100	**1.2**	**15.757**
Manipur	3180	**0.04**	8382	**0.05**	18277	**0.05**	45944	**0.06**	97200	**0.06**	**18.648**
Arunachal Pradesh	-	-	-	-	32305	**0.1**	53745	**0.07**	108200	**0.07**	**12.848**
Meghalaya	12670	**0.17**	27275	**0.18**	65429	**0.19**	140283	**0.19**	290600	**0.19**	**16.957**

STATE/REGION	1985	%age	1990	%age	1995	%age	2000	%age	2005	%age	G.R.(%)
Mizoram	-	-	-	-	18009	**0.05**	32136	**0.04**	72200	**0.05**	**14.896**
Nagaland	7685	**0.1**	18053	**0.12**	30002	**0.09**	76967	**0.11**	128300	**0.08**	**15.114**
Tripura	9523	**0.13**	23054	**0.15**	48887	**0.15**	127363	**0.18**	265100	**0.18**	**18.095**
EASTERN	***1371048***	***18.09***	***2755547***	***18.08***	***4875811***	***14.53***	***11038616***	***15.27***	***20728700***	***13.71***	***14.545***
Bihar	381828	**5.04**	825302	**5.41**	1527408	**4.55**	3740345	**5.17**	6863300	**4.54**	**15.54**
Orissa	102571	**1.35**	234951	**1.54**	527523	**1.57**	1274401	**1.76**	2667700	**1.76**	**17.694**
Sikkim	-	-	10646	**0.07**	14703	**0.04**	46259	**0.06**	126100	**0.08**	**17.915**
West Bengal	886649	**11.7**	1684648	**11.05**	2806177	**8.36**	5977611	**8.27**	11071600	**7.32**	**13.455**
CENTRAL	***1158716***	***15.29***	***2447556***	***16.06***	***4944747***	***14.73***	***11356328***	***15.7***	***21883900***	***14.47***	***15.826***
Madhya Pradesh	304266	**4.01**	657290	**4.31**	1338697	**3.99**	3088838	**4.27**	6372800	**4.21**	**16.427**
Uttar Pradesh	854450	**11.27**	1790266	**11.75**	3606050	**10.74**	8267490	**11.43**	15511100	**10.26**	**15.597**
WESTERN	***2168538***	***28.61***	***4298453***	***28.2***	***10603754***	***31.59***	***20503024***	***28.35***	***49360800***	***32.64***	***16.912***
Goa	-	-	-	-	274998	**0.82**	651837	**0.9**	1154800	**0.76**	**15.43**
Gujarat	532562	**7.03**	1018202	**6.68**	2344573	**6.99**	4832709	**6.68**	9767100	**6.46**	**15.656**

Maharashtra	1635976	**21.59**	3280251	**21.52**	7984183	**23.79**	15018478	**20.77**	38438900	**25.42**	**17.098**
SOUTHERN	*1791071*	*23.63*	*3530043*	*23.16*	*8293374*	*24.71*	*18648977*	*25.79*	*38873300*	*25.71*	*16.634*
Andhra Pradesh	486799	**6.42**	935357	**6.14**	2017765	**6.01**	4635925	**6.41**	9852600	**6.52**	**16.228**
Karnataka	424547	**5.6**	821804	**5.39**	1969942	5.87	4591065	**6.35**	10941700	**7.24**	**17.641**
Kerala	342422	**4.52**	649757	**4.26**	1725008	**5.14**	3904494	**5.4**	7046100	**4.66**	**16.324**
Tamil Nadu	537303	**7.09**	1123125	**7.37**	2580659	7.69	5517493	**7.63**	11032900	**7.3**	**16.312**
TOTAL DEPOSITS	*7578936*	*100*	*15242002*	*100*	*33561985*	*100*	*72312169*	*100*	*151206400*	*100*	*16.14*
MEAN	**394090.4**		**781911.9**		**1736753.2**		**3434752.8**		**8139462.6**		**16.346**

Source : Same as for Table 4.1

Note : ----- indicates nil.

The total deposits witnessed the highest growth rate in those state, which accounted for the lowest proportion of deposits. The total deposits went up at the highest rate in Manipur (18.648%) followed by Tripura (18.095%) and Sikkim (17.915%). On the contrary they went up at the lowest rate in Arunachal Pradesh (12.848%) followed by West Bengal (13.455%) and Punjab (14.386%).

Per Capita Scheduled Commercial Bank Deposits in India

Despite the drastic reduction in effective rate of interest on deposits during 1990s, per capita deposits has gone up at a considerable rate in India. Table 4.5 brings into light that per capita deposits in India, which stood at Rs. 998 in the year 1985 went up to Rs. 16032 in the year 2005, registering a growth rate of 14.894 per cent per year.

Among different regions, Western region stood at the top throughout the reference period. Besides this, Northern region and Southern region also witnessed high per capita deposits during most of the years under study. On the contrary, the North Eastern region followed by the Central region registered the lower per capita deposits in all the years under reference.

It is evident from the table that Punjab stood the highest with respect to per capita deposits during the year 1985 and 1990, but during the later period under study, this position was occupied by the newly carved state of Goa. Besides these two states; Kerala, Himachal Pradesh and West Bengal also registered high per capita deposits in most of the years under study. In contrast to it, Manipur witnessed the lowest per capita deposits throughout the period under study. Apart from it, Orissa, Tripura, Assam and Bihar also registered low per capita deposits during the reference period. Thus, in most of the cases, the states having a sound industrial, agricultural, business and tourism base witnessed high per capita deposits and vice-versa.

The per capita deposits went up at a rate of more than 10 per cent per annum in all states (except Nagaland) during the reference period. The public sector image of banking system, combined with the absence of any effective social security system for the populace and fluctuating nature of investment opportunities in the capital market, have retained the attractive nature bank deposits.

TABLE 4.5

Per Capita Deposits in India

(Amt. in Rs.)

STATE/REGION	*1985*	*1990*	*1995*	*2000*	*2005*	*G.R.(%)*
NORTHERN	***1178***	***2125***	***4120***	***8173***	***13548***	***12.989***
Haryana	1091	2138	4115	8291	15850	14.32
Himachal Pradesh	1182	2361	4976	10402	18926	14.872
Jammu & Kashmir	1254	2046	4229	8786	15561	13.422
Punjab	2484	4355	8199	16208	25285	12.301
Rajasthan	573	1073	2180	4309	6897	13.25
NORTH EASTERN	***473***	***900***	***1782***	***3501***	***6633***	***14.116***
Assam	458	852	1647	3225	6335	14.041
Manipur	202	468	896	1975	3665	15.597
Arunachal Pradesh	-	-	3397	5018	8972	10.199
Meghalaya	846	1581	3320	6246	11352	13.861
Mizoram		-	2357	3698	7315	11.991
Nagaland	830	1560	2033	4066	5289	9.702
Tripura	412	861	1672	4050	7834	15.862
EASTERN	***834***	***1509***	***2416***	***4955***	***8424***	***12.259***
Bihar	502	976	1607	3490	5679	2.898
Orissa	362	756	1570	3524	6850	15.845
Sikkim	-	2688	3231	8811	20843	14.63
West Bengal	1487	2530	3860	7575	12924	11.418
CENTRAL	***648***	***1220***	***2206***	***4540***	***7838***	***13.273***
Madhya Pradesh	530	10171	1864	3883	7234	13.958
Uttar Pradesh	704	1316	2367	4846	8116	13.004
WESTERN	***2053***	***3653***	***8053***	***14071***	***30611***	***14.465***
Goa	-	-	22231	49195	81267	13.84
Gujarat	1447	2513	5233	9747	17800	13.371
Maharashtra	2378	4252	9324	15842	36623	14.652
SOUTHERN	***1014***	***1829***	***4017***	***8490***	***16229***	***14.871***
Andhra Pradesh	834	1437	2880	6202	12352	14.43
Karnataka	1059	1862	4110	8846	19470	15.671
Kerala	1275	2263	5718	12374	21348	15.13
Tamil Nadu	1048	2040	4428	8978	17025	14.956
MEAN	998	1861	4298	8783	16032	14.898
SD	**601.184**	**1023.271**	**4251.664**	**9234.262**	**15343.94**	
CV (%)	**60.244**	**54.981**	**98.926**	**105.132**	**95.705**	
HI (%)	**6.408**	**5.857**	**7.758**	**8.244**	**7.646**	

Sources : i. Same as for Table 4.2

The per capita deposits in the highest ranking state were nearly twelve times more than the lowest ranking state in 1985, but in 2005 the difference between the two increased to twenty two times. This reflects an increase in inter-state disparities during the reference period. This fact is further corroborated by the values of co-efficient of variation and Herfindahl Index. The values of co-efficient of variation and Herfindahl Index were 60.24 per cent and 6.408 per cent in 1985, which went up to an alarming level of 95.705 per cent and 7.646 per cent respectively, in the year 2005.

Bank Deposits Per 10,000 Square Kms. of Area

In an economy one of the apt way to measure deposit mobilization is in terms of deposit per 10,000 sq. kms. of area.[1] The scheduled commercial bank deposit per 10,000 square kms. of area have been depicted in Table 4.6. It is evident from the table that these deposits were merely Rs. 28 thousand in the year 1985, which went up to Rs. 590 thousand in the year 2005. Thus, deposits per 10,000 square kms. of area in India, went up by more than 20 times showing a growth rate of 16.424 per cent per annum during the period under context.

It is clear from the table that Western region, as in case of per capita deposits with respect to deposits per 10,000 square kms. of area also stood at the top throughout the period. On the contrary, the North-Eastern region not only witnessed the lowest deposits per 10,000 square kms. of area, but also the lowest per annum increase in there deposits.

The state-wise analysis reveals that West Bengal witnessed the highest deposits per 10,000 square kms. of area in 1985 and 1990. But, during the later period this position was occupied by Goa, mainly due to its small geographical area. Besides these states; Punjab, Kerala and Maharastra also showed high deposits per 10,000 square kms. of area. As against this, all the North Eastern states(except Assam and Tripura) and Jammu & Kashmir, registered the lowest amount of these in most of the years under study.

The deposits per 10,000 square kms. of area registered the highest growth rate in Manipur (18.648%), followed by Tripura (18.095%) and Sikkim (17.915%). On the other hand, these deposits

TABLE 4.6

Deposits per 10,000 Square Kms in India

STATE/REGION	*1985*	*1990*	*1995*	*2000*	*2005*	*G.R.(%)*
NORTHERN	***13426.367***	***27206.676***	***58853.321***	***131222.486***	***244399.921***	***15.613***
Haryana	35116.484	77716.683	169163.123	385715.19	834434.09	17.164
Himachal Pradesh	9804.034	21513.84	49290.141	111734.773	220358.163	16.839
Jammu & Kashmir	3738.458	6926.331	15976.254	37915.295	76013.484	16.255
Punjab	89320.122	172111.91	355119.733	768740.519	1313391.049	14.386
Rajasthan	6336.122	13453.405	31030.771	69655.504	126584.054	16.152
NORTH EASTERN	***8648.467***	***17694.913***	***23854.824***	***51781.342***	***108580.344***	***13.486***
Assam	12352.814	24110.508	50433.081	107653.816	230513.272	15.757
Manipur	1424.284	3754.199	8186.053	20577.776	43534.734	18.848
Arunachal Pradesh	-	-	3857.636	6417.85	12920.483	12.848
Meghalaya	5648.937	12160.596	29171.608	62545.365	12964.403	16.957
Mizoram	-	-	8542.764	15244.059	34248.85	14.896
Nagaland	4635.382	10889.077	18096.387	46424.392	77387.056	15.114
Tripura	9081.633	21985.509	46621.209	121460.042	252813.275	18.095
EASTERN	***32787.955***	***64797.979***	***114656.98***	***259578.227***	***487445.091***	***14.449***
Bihar	21959.661	47464.702	87844.166	215114.42	394721.556	15.54
Orissa	6587.437	15089.302	33879.209	81846.096	171328.2	17.694
Sikkim	-	15002.818	20720.124	65190.248	177705.75	17.915
West Bengal	99901.861	189815.215	316181.833	673518.456	1247476.113	13.455
CENTRAL	***15703.802***	***33171.143***	***67014.97***	***153909.606***	***296587.279***	***15.826***
Madhya Pradesh	6861.399	14822.323	38188.501	69655.336	143710.846	16.427
Uttar Pradesh	29022.353	60808.394	122483.535	280814.576	526851.918	15.597
WESTERN	***43050.977***	***85335.19***	***208966.083***	***404049.038***	***972743.522***	***16.869***
Goa	-	-	742836.305	1760769.854	3119394.922	15.43
Gujarat	27168.204	51942.721	119606.426	246536.598	498260.417	15.656
Maharashtra	53169.619	106608.957	259468.498	488067.712	1249180.243	17.098
SOUTHERN	***28171.238***	***55523.027***	***130448.804***	***293334.985***	***611449.029***	***16.635***
Andhra Pradesh	17697.406	34004.573	73361.268	168551.51	358217.746	16.228
Karnataka	22135.919	42848.935	1022712.953	239378.542	570501.223	17.641
Kerala	88110.028	167191.673	509407.908	1153026.607	2080766.618	17.128
Tamil Nadu	41312.568	86355.703	198423.703	424233.265	848306.14	16.312
MEAN	28161.177	54389.88	173224.128	304831.512	589527.384	16.424
SD	30192.464	56794.03	251959.978	411176.029	737668.315	
CV(%)	107.213	104.42	145.453	134.886	125.128	
HI(%)	9.975	9.276	12.124	10.987	10.012	

Sources : **i.** Same as for Table 4.1

increased at the lowest rate in Arunachal Pradesh (12.848%). It was followed by West Bengal (13.455%), Punjab (14.386%) and Mizoram (14.896%).

The inter-state disparities with respect to deposits per 10,000 square kms. of area, which already were at a high level went up to a more alarming level during the period under study. In 1985, the values of co-efficient of variation (C.V) and Herfindahl Index (H.I) were 107.21 and 9.98 per cent, but in 2005 they went up to 125.13 and 10.01 per cent respectively.

Scheduled Commercial Bank Deposits Per Branch in India

It is clear from Table 4.7 that bank deposits per branch, which were just Rs. 129.66 lacs in 1985 rose to Rs. 2009.41 lacs in 2005. Thus, these deposits registered an annual compound growth rate of 14.687 per cent, per annum.

Region-wise analysis reveals that Western region remained at the top, with respect to this indicator, throughout the period under context. On the other hand, in North-Eastern region deposits per branch remained minimum in all the years under reference. The Western region (15.306%), followed by the Southern region (15.234%) registered the highest increase in deposits per branch. On the contrary, Eastern region showed the lowest growth rate(13.05%). It was followed by the Northern region (13.957%).

The table further reveals that Maharastra ranked the highest with respect to deposits per branch in all the years under study. It was followed by Goa during the period 1995-2005. Apart from these two states; West Bengal, Punjab and Gujarat also registered high deposits per branch in most of the years under study. On the other hand, Manipur in 1985 and 1995, Orissa in 1990 and Mizoram in rest of the years under study were placed at the bottom, with respect to deposits per branch. Besides these states Tripura and Rajasthan also registered low deposits per branch in most of the years under context.

Deposits per branch registered the highest growth rate in Manipur (17.294%), followed by Tripura (16.387%) and Orissa (16.077%). On the contrary, West Bengal showed the lowest growth rate (11.699%). It was followed by Punjab (12.656%), Sikkim (12.989%) and Arunachal Pradesh (13.013%).

TABLE 4.7

Deposits per Branch in India

(Rs. Lacs)

STATE/REGION	*1985*	*1990*	*1995*	*2000*	*2005*	*G.R.(%)*
NORTHERN	***136.561.***	***247.678***	***501.635***	***1045.309***	***1862.755***	***13.957***
Haryana	140.887	273.568	547.915	1130.851	2211.751	14.761
Himachal Pradesh	100.15	172.337	356.844	790.421	1535.419	14.625
Jammu & Kashmir	114.438	206.338	450.419	1041.804	2013.17	15.416
Punjab	225.142	406.752	782.693	1593.439	2440.775	12.658
Rajasthan	81.647	152.308	329.914	708.435	1271.185	14.713
NORTH EASTERN	***97.561***	***168.707***	***314.794***	***683.318***	***1460.042***	***14.487***
Assam	102.859	166.331	313.958	668.679	1464.049	14.2
Manipur	51.29	123.265	207.693	522.091	1246.154	17.294
Arunachal Pradesh	-	-	468.188	778.913	1591.176	13.013
Meghalaya	99.764	189.41	363.494	775.044	1587.978	14.84
Mizoram	-	-	227.962	406.785	913.924	14.896
Nagaland	118.231	261.638	416.694	1099.529	1781.944	14.527
Tripura	70.022	145.911	264.254	695.973	1456.593	16.387
EASTERN	***149.612***	***260.991***	***420.437***	***927.927***	***1739.27***	***13.05***
Bihar	92.296	179.452	306.401	736.578	1351.842	4.363
Orissa	59.668	120.86	242.094	567.157	1176.753	16.077
Sikkim	-	367.103	350.071	1005.63	2292.727	12.989
West Bengal	268.032	422.641	639.075	132.019	2450.011	11.699
CENTRAL	***105.693***	***195.429***	***372.261***	***833.492***	***1595.502***	***14.536***
Madhya Pradesh	82.368	153.501	298.084	677.08	1406.178	15.243
Uttar Pradesh	117.547	217.213	410.151	912.224	1688.926	14.254
WESTERN	***272.841***	***486.856***	***1080.472***	***1954.717***	***4709.101***	***15.306***
Goa	-	-	989201	2018.071	3416.568	13.196
Gujarat	173.529	305.675	653.995	1294.938	2636.194	14.572
Maharashtra	335.31	596.626	1341.654	2334.237	5969.7	15.485
SOUTHERN	***122.091***	***222.73***	***481.809***	***1019.627***	***2081.012***	***15.234***
Andhra Pradesh	118.358	206.298	410.282	887.089	1826.924	14.664
Karnataka	108.719	194.418	435.539	948.567	2211.338	16.257
Kerala	125.89	230.084	553.064	1176.761	2017.206	14.878
Tamil Nadu	136.649	263.397	554.623	1124.6242	2276.702	15.103
MEAN	129.657	243.415	476.57	1005.674	2009.407	14.687
SD	**69.557**	**116.239**	**256.634**	**444.71**	**996.99**	
CV (%)	53.647	47.753	53.85	44.22	49.616	
HI (%)	6.067	5.535	5.114	4.751	4.945	

Sources : **i.** compued from Table 4.1 and 4.4.

The value of co-efficient of variation (C.V) and Herfindahl Index (H.I) reveal that the inter-state disparities with respect to this indicator declined over a period of time. The values of co-efficient of variation (C.V) and Herfindahl Index (H.I), which were 53.647 per cent and 6.067 per cent in 1985, came down to 49.616 per cent and 4.945 per cent respectively, in 2005.

Credit Deployment in India

Credit deployment is one of the basic activities of commercial banks. Credit is so inextricably interlinked with banking that a preliminary survey of banks cannot be completed without an analysis of the nature and use of credit.[2] It plays a vital role in the upliftment of a country.[3] The Indian banking system has acquired a wide reach not only with respect to deposit mobilization, but in credit deployment also. It is evident from Table 4.8 that total credit deployed by commercial banks in India, which was to the tune of Rs. 49948 crores in 1985, went up to the Rs. 1002399 crores in 2005, registering an annual growth rate of 16.179 per cent. The average credit per state also went up by more than 20 times during the period under reference.

Among different regions, western region (comprising three state viz. Goa, Gujarat and Maharastra), accounted for a very huge share in total credit deployed by scheduled commercial banks. It's share always stood more than 31 per cent. The western region was followed by southern region, which accounted for more than 29 per cent of total credit deployed in the country. In sharp contrast to it, the North-Eastern region account for nearly one per cent share in the total credit deployed.

The state wise analysis reveals that Maharastra, followed by Tamil-Nadu, always accounted for a lion's share in total credit deployed by commercial banks. The individual share of these states always stood more than 25 per cent and 10 per cent respectively. Beside these two states West Bengal, Andhra Pradesh and Uttar Pradesh also enjoyed a large volume of commercial banks credit during most of the years. On the contrary; Himachal Pradesh, Sikkim, Goa and all the North-Eastern states (except Assam), witnessed a very low amount of total credit of commercial banks. The individual share of all these state like total deposit, in total credit also always stood less than one per cent.

TABLE 4.8
TOTAL CREDIT IN INDIA

(Rs. Lacs.)

STATE/REGION	1985	%age	1990	%age	1995	%age	2000	%age	2005	%age	G.R.(%)
NORTHERN	*513922*	*10.29*	*986007*	*9.66*	*1761988*	*9.42*	*3796083*	*9.49*	*9039000*	*9.02*	*15.415*
Haryana	106045	**2.12**	210250	**2.06**	340650	**1.82**	722307	**1.81**	1916300	**1.91**	**15.571**
Himachal Pradesh	22663	**0.45**	46200	**0.45**	71261	**0.38**	147768	**0.37**	442000	**0.44**	**16.013**
Jammu & Kashmir	33892	**0.68**	48931	**0.48**	103901	**0.56**	288257	**0.72**	667300	**0.67**	**16.068**
Punjab	205077	**4.11**	394312	**3.86**	740098	**3.96**	1524386	**3.81**	3024200	**3.02**	**14.402**
Rajasthan	146245	**2.93**	286314	**2.81**	506078	**2.71**	1113365	**2.78**	2989200	**2.98**	**16.285**
NORTH EASTERN	*66130*	*1.32*	*141906*	*1.39*	*216379*	*1.16*	*370619*	*0.93*	*964500*	*0.96*	*14.339*
Assam	50731	**1.02**	104994	**1.03**	153024	**0.82**	270116	**0.68**	621900	**0.62**	**13.35**
Manipur	2284	**0.05**	5861	**0.06**	10636	**0.06**	17204	**0.04**	39800	**0.04**	**15.361**
Arunachal Pradesh	-	-	-	-	4017	**0.02**	8426	**0.02**	26400	**0.03**	**20.717**
Meghalaya	3531	**0.07**	6721	**0.07**	11142	**0.06**	22862	**0.06**	131600	**0.13**	**19.831**
Mizoram					2969	**0.02**	7475	**0.02**	36800	**0.04**	**28.625**

STATE/REGION	*1985*	*%age*	*1990*	*%age*	*1995*	*%age*	*2000*	*%age*	*2005*	*%age*	*G.R.(%)*
Nagaland	2883	**0.06**	7689	**0.08**	11353	**0.06**	11805	**0.03**	29400	**0.03**	**12.312**
Tripura	6701	**0.13**	16641	**0.16**	23238	**0.12**	32731	**0.08**	78600	**0.08**	**13.1**
EASTERN	***687329***	***13.76***	***4033636***	***39.53***	***2299596***	***12.3***	***4094803***	***10.24***	***9610100***	***9.59***	***14.098***
Bihar	151975	**3.04**	330408	**3.24**	496438	**2.66**	839907	**2.1**	1983200	**1.98**	**13.705**
Orissa	88978	**1.78**	191085	**1.87**	287573	**1.54**	529269	**1.32**	1659100	**1.66**	**15.752**
Sikkim	-	-	3013	**0.03**	3534	**0.02**	6982	**0.02**	36500	**0.04**	**18.092**
West Bengal	446376	**8.94**	924458	**9.06**	1512051	**8.09**	2718645	**6.8**	5931300	**5.92**	**13.808**
CENTRAL	***580803***	***11.63***	***1292336***	***12.67***	***1929024***	***10.32***	***3847500***	***9.62***	***8873400***	***8.85***	***14.605***
Madhya Pradesh	183760	**3.68**	450939	**4.42**	663359	**3.55**	1516374	**3.79**	3376500	**3.37**	**15.667**
Uttar Pradesh	397043	**7.95**	841397	**8.25**	1265665	**6.77**	2331126	**5.83**	5496900	**5.48**	**14.042**
WESTERN	***1681324***	***33.66***	***3238343***	***31.74***	***6711883***	***35.9***	***15498108***	***38.74***	***41448000***	***41.35***	***17.38***
Goa	-	-	-	-	67921	**0.36**	155213	**0.39**	291200	**0.29**	**15.669**
Gujarat	289808	**5.8**	623822	**6.11**	1092991	**5.85**	2367981	**5.92**	4564300	**4.55**	**14.779**

Maharashtra	1391516	**27.86**	2614521	**25.63**	5550971	**29.69**	12974914	**32.44**	36592500	**36.5**	**17.759**
SOUTHERN	***1465301***	*29.34*	***3095416***	*30.34*	***5776296***	*30.9*	***12395604***	*30.99*	***30304900***	*30.23*	*16.353*
Andhra Pradesh	375880	**7.53**	815142	**7.99**	1472382	**7.88**	2977888	**7.44**	7398700	**7.38**	**16.066**
Karnataka	367684	**7.36**	747626	**7.33**	1295556	**6.93**	2907938	**7.27**	8110600	**8.09**	**16.729**
Kerala	217475	**4.35**	415751	**4.07**	772991	**4.13**	1621489	**4.05**	3935100	**3.93**	**15.579**
Tamil Nadu	504262	**10.1**	1116897	**10.95**	2235367	**11.96**	4888289	**12.22**	10860500	**10.83**	**16.59**
TOTAL CREDIT	***4994809***	***100***	***10202972***	***100***	***18695166***	***100***	***40002717***	***100***	***100239900***	***100***	*16.179*
MEAN	**237848.05**		**463771.46**		**747806.64**		**1600108.7**		**4009596**		**15.170**

Source : Same as for Table 4.1

Note : ----- indicates nil.

The total credit registered the highest increase in Mizoram (28.625%), followed by Arunachal Pradesh (20.717%) and Meghalaya (19.831%). On the other hand, it went up at the lowest rate in Nagaland (12.312%). It was followed by Tripura (13.1%), Assam (13.35%) and Bihar (13.705%).

Per Capita Scheduled Commercial Bank Credit in India

Table 4.9 throws light up on the fact that per capita credit, which stood at Rs. 598 in 1985, went up to Rs. 7891 in the year in 2005. It increased by more than fourteen times, exhibited an annual compound growth rate of 13.767 per cent.

The regions wise analysis reveals that the western region not only witnessed the maximum per capita credit but also the fastest growth in it during the reference period. In contrast to it, North-Eastern region registered minimum per capita credit throughout the period under context.

The table further elicits that Maharastra not only enjoyed the highest volume of overall credit, but per capita credit also, during all the years under context. It was followed by Goa during the period 1995-2005. Beside these two states; Tamil Nadu, Karnataka and Punjab also ranked high with respect to this indicator. Punjab, which ranked second in 1985 with respect to per capita credit, slid down to third position in 1990, to fourth position in 1995 and ultimately to sixth position in 2005. On the other hand Bihar, Orissa and all the North-Eastern states witnessed very low per capita credit in most of the years.

It is further evident form the table that some of the North-Eastern states succeeded to improve their position with respect to this indicator. The per capita credit increased at the highest rate in Mizoram (25.372%) followed in descending order by Arunachal Pradesh (17.884%) and Meghalaya (16.656%). On the other hand, Nagaland (7.03%) followed by, Tripura (10.962%) Bihar (11.105%) and Uttar Pradesh (11.484%) witnessed the lowest rate of growth in per capita credit.

The inter-state variations with respect to per capita credit, widened further during period under context. The values of coefficient of variation (C.V) and Herfindabl index (H.I) were respectively, 72.76 per cent and 7.16 per cent in 1985, but they

TABLE 4.9
Per Capita Credit in India

(Amount in Rs.)

STATE/REGION	*1985*	*1990*	*1995*	*2000*	*2005*	*G.R.(%)*
NORTHERN	***631***	***1078***	***1714***	***2420***	***6962***	***12.756***
Haryana	745	1308	1874	3512	8233	12.765
Himachal Pradesh	491	911	1292	2471	6819	14.06
Jammu & Kashmir	511	650	1210	2940	6012	13.113
Punjab	1133	1981	3393	6382	11560	12.317
Rajasthan	386	667	1039	2013	4759	13.38
NORTH EASTERN	***241***	***480***	***634***	***982***	***2310***	***11.972***
Assam	240	473	637	1032	2179	11.67
Manipur	145	327	521	740	1501	12.394
Arunachal Pradesh	-	-	422	787	2189	17.884
Meghalaya	236	390	565	1018	5141	16.656
Mizoram	-	-	389	860	3728	25.372
Nagaland	311	665	769	624	1212	7.038
Tripura	390	622	795	1041	2323	10.962
EASTERN	***418***	***793***	***1139***	***1838***	***3906***	***11.821***
Bihar	200	391	522	784	1641	11.105
Orissa	314	615	856	1463	4260	13.933
Sikkim	-	761	777	1330	6033	14.802
West Bengal	749	1388	2080	3445	6923	11.763
CENTRAL	***325***	***644***	***861***	***1538***	***3178***	***12.079***
Madhya Pradesh	320	698	924	1906	3833	13.215
Uttar Pradesh	327	619	831	1366	2876	11.484
WESTERN	***1592***	***2752***	***5098***	***10636***	***25704***	***14.922***
Goa	-	-	5491	11714	20493	14.077
Gujarat	787	1539	2440	4776	8318	12.511
Maharastra	2022	3389	6482	13686	34864	15.299
SOUTHERN	***830***	***1604***	***2798***	***5643***	***12963***	***14.733***
Andhra Pradesh	644	1252	2102	3984	9276	14.271
Karnatka	917	1694	2703	5603	14432	14.775
Kerala	810	1448	2562	5139	11922	14.393
Tamil Nadu	984	2028	3835	7954	16759	15.231
MEAN	598	1083	1780	3463	7891	13.768
SD	435.197	732.696	1596.045	3438.449	7524.798	
CV(%)	72.775	67.654	89.665	99.291	95.359	
HI(%)	7.163	6.533	7.086	7.786	7.491	

Sources : **i.** Same as for Table 4.12

went up to 95.35 per cent and 7.49 per cent in 2005.

Bank Credit per 10,000 Square Kms. of Area In India

Table 4.10 shows that credit per 10,000 square kilometers of area in India, which stood at 15 thousand in 1985, increased to 304 thousand in 2005. Thus it went up by more than 20 times showing a growth rate of 16.375 per cent per annum during the period under context.

The table further brings in to light that western region, as in case of per capita credit, with respect to credit per 10,000 square kilometers of area also, stood at the top in all the years under reference. It was followed by the southern region. In contrast to it, the North-Eastern region, not only showed the lowest credit per 10,000 square kilometers of area, but also the lowest per annum increase in it.

The state-wise analysis elaborates that West-Bengal witnessed the highest credit per 10,000 square kilometers of area in 1985, but during the later period this position, was occupied by Kerala for the years 1990,1995 and 2005. Maharastra also stood at the top in the year 2000. Beside these states; Tamil Nadu, Punjab and Goa also showed high credit per 10,000 square kilometers of area. In contrast to it, all the North-Eastern states (except Assam and Tripura) and Jammu & Kashmir registered the lowest amount of credit in most of the years under study.

The credit per 10,000 square kilometers of area registered the highest growth rate in Kerala (38.247%). It was followed by Mizoram (28.625%), Arunachal Pradesh (20.717%) and Meghalaya (19.831%). On the contrary, this credit increased at the lowest rate in Nagaland (12.312%), followed by Tripura (13.1%), Assam (13.5%) and Bihar (13.705%).

The inter-state disparities with respect to credit per 10,000 square kilometers of area in India, reflected by the value of co-efficient of variations (C.V) widened further during the period under study. This value, which already was at a high level of 108.15 per cent in 1985, went up to 119.54 per cent in 2005.

Scheduled Commercial Bank Credit Per Branch in India

A close perusal of the data presented in Table 4.11 brings

TABLE 4.10

Credit per 10,000 Square Kms of area in India

(Rs. Lakhs)

STATE/REGION	1985	1990	1995	2000	2005	G.R.(%)
NORTHERN	7190.516	13795.67	24481.51	38849.486	125590.158	15.374
Haryana	23985.57	47554.96	77049.22	163373.519	433434.362	15.571
Himachal Pradesh	4070.734	8298.457	12799.92	26542.13	79392.165	16.013
Jammu & Kashmir	1525.045	2201.758	4572.383	12685.358	29365.946	15.939
Punjab	40720.58	78295.54	146955.6	302685.755	600492.435	14.402
Rajasthan	4273.183	8365.908	14787.27	32531.798	87342.435	16.285
NORTH EASTERN	4401.067	9444.093	8482.69	14529.349	37811.222	11.353
Assam	6467.656	13385.6	19508.91	34436.88	79285.55	13.35
Manipur	1022.977	2625.073	4763.739	7705.469	17825.951	15.361
Arunachal Pradesh	--	--	479.682	1006.174	3152.502	20.717
Meghalaya	1574.301	2996567	4967.676	10193.054	58674.038	19.831
Mizoram	--	--	1408.377	3545.847	17456. 477	28.625
Nagaland	1738.947	4637.795	6847.82	7120 454	17733.277	12.312
Tripura	6390.425	15869.73	22160.98	31213.1	74957.086	13.1
EASTERN	16437.14	34073.07	54076.08	96291.211	225986.004	14.002
Bihar	8740.374	19002.4	28551.1	48304.664	114057.638	13.705
Orissa	5714.451	12272.09	18468.86	33991.343	106552.692	15.752
Sikkim	--	4246.054	4980.271	9838.346	51437.43	18.092

STATE/REGION	1985	1990	1995	2000	2005	G.R.(%)
West Bengal	50294.75	104161.9	170368.1	306319.294	668300.433	13.808
CENTRAL	7871.485	17514.72	26143.6	52144.237	120259.075	14.605
Madhya Pradesh	4143.909	10168.97	14959.18	34195.235	76142.304	15.667
Uttar Pradesh	13486.01	28578.99	42989.73	79179.311	186708.377	14.042
WESTERN	33378.54	64289.32	132269.8	305418.149	816807.538	17.336
Goa	--	--	183471.1	419267.963	786601.837	15.669
Gujarat	14784.31	31823.76	55785.02	120800.565	232843.938	14.759
Maharashtra	45224.61	84972.57	180394.4	421656.349	1189176.28	17.759
SOUTHERN	23047.3	48686.9	90856.98	194973.929	476674.264	16.354
Andhra Pradesh	13664.99	29634.2	53532.4	108269.12	268999.618	16.067
Karnataka	19171.08	38981.29	67550.41	151620.149	422887.414	16.729
Kerala	1787.01	106978.6	228270.1	478837.965	1162064.79	38.247
Tamil Nadu	38772.09	85876.84	171874.6	375854.542	835050.516	16.59
MEAN	14645.38	33678.6	61499.88	128846.975	303997.42	16.375
SD	15839.58	35050.98	72174.32	156241.526	363402.512	
CV (%)	108.154	104.075	117.357	121.261	119.541	
HI (%)	10.067	9.245	9.289	9.646	9.487	

Sources : **i.** Same as for Table 4.1

into light that credit per branch in India, which was to the tune of Rs. 78.83 lacs in 1985, increased to Rs. 1059.90 lacs in 2005. Thus, credit per branch in India increased by more than 13 times showing a compound growth rate of 13.875 per cent per annum.

Among different regions, Western region not only stood at the top with respect to credit per branch throughout the period under study, but also showed the highest growth rate (15.767%) in it. On the other hand, North-Eastern region witnessed the lowest credit per branch in all the years under context. It also showed the lowest growth rate(12.609%) in credit per branch.

The table further elaborates that commercial banks deployed the highest credit per branch in Maharastra throughout the period under reference. It was followed by West Bengal in the year 1985. But during the later period Tamil Nadu occupied this position. Apart from these states, Punjab and Gujarat also registered high credit per branch in most of the years under study. On the other hand, Meghalaya in 1985 and 1990, Mizoram in 1995 and 2000 and Arunachal Pradesh in 2005 remained at the bottom with respect to credit per branch. Besides these states; Manipur, Himachal Pradesh and Bihar also witnessed low credit per branch in most of the years under reference.

Credit per branch registered the highest growth rate in Mizoram (28.625%) followed by Arunachal Pradesh (20.894%), Meghalaya (17.662%) and Maharastra (16.137%). In contrast to it, Tripura (11.465%) witnessed the lowest growth rate in credit per branch. It was followed by Nagaland (11.739%), Assam (11.826%) and West Bengal (12.047%).

The values of co-efficient of variation (C.V) and Herfindahl Index (H.I) reveal that the inter-state disparities with respect to this indicator increased over a period of time. The value of co-efficient of variation (C.V) and Herfindahl Index (H.I), which were 71.567 per cent and 7.085 per cent in 1985, went up to 100.246 per cent and 7.859 per cent in 2005.

Credit-Deposit Ratio

One more important indicator of the growth of banking in a particular state/area is the credit deposit ratio.[4] This ratio shows that how much of the resources mobilized in a particular

TABLE 4.11
Credit per Branch in India

STATE/REGION	*1985*	*1990*	*1995*	*2000*	*2005*	*G.R.(%)*
NORTHERN	***73.135***	***125.59***	***208.667***	***309.472***	***957.217***	***13.722***
Haryana	96.23	167.396	249.56	478.983	1148.861	13.2
Himachal Pradesh	41.584	66.475	92.667	187.761	553.191	13.814
Jammu & Kashmir	46.683	65.591	128.909	348.557	777.739	15.102
Punjab	102.641	185.036	323.894	598.268	1115.941	12.672
Rajasthan	55.062	94.712	157.216	330.886	877.113	14.844
NORTH EASTERN	***49.647***	***90.042***	***111.939***	***191.733***	***508.434***	***12.336***
Assam	53.855	92.343	121.448	213.869	503.563	11.826
Manipur	36.839	86.191	120.864	195.5	510.256	14.044
Arunachal Pradesh	-	-	58.217	122.116	388.235	20.894
Meghalaya	27.803	46.674	61.9	126.309	719.126	17.662
Mizoram	-	-	37.582	94.62	465.823	28.625
Nagaland	44.354	111.435	157.681	168.643	408.333	11.739
Tripura	49.272	105.323	125.611	178.858	431.868	11.465
EASTERN	***75.003***	***137.238***	***198.292***	***344.217***	***806.352***	***12.609***
Bihar	36.736	71.843	99.586	165.401	390.624	12.547
Orissa	51.762	98.295	131.975	235.545	731.848	14.162
Sikkim	-	103.897	84.143	151.783	663.636	13.159
West Bengal	134.938	231.926	344.352	600.806	1312.526	12.047

CENTRAL	***52.978***	***103.189***	***145.225***	***282.385***	***646.938***	***13.328***
Madhya Pradesh	49.7455	105.31	147.709	332.392	745.035	13.491
Uttar Pradesh	54.621	102.087	143.956	257.214	598.53	12.716
WESTERN	***211.541***	***366.785***	***683.909***	***1477.558***	***3954.207***	***15.767***
Goa	-	-	244.32	480.536	861.538	13.431
Gujarat	94.431	187.278	304.879	634.507	1231.93	13.703
Maharashtra	285.205	475.54	932.78	2016.617	5682.948	16.137
SOUTHERN	***99.885***	***195.307***	***335.578***	***677.726***	***1622.318***	***14.956***
Andhra Pradesh	91.388	179.784	299.386	569/822	1371/908	14.504
Karnataka	94.157	176.869	286.437	600.814	1639.167	15.358
Kerala	79.954	147.221	247.833	488.695	1126.567	14.142
Tamil Nadu	128.246	291.936	480.414	996.39	2241.127	15.378
MEAN	78.834	145.144	215.333	422.996	1059.897	13.875
SD	56.419	95.31	184.695	399.254	1062.508	
CV (%)	71.567	65.668	85.772	94.387	100.246	
HI (%)	7.085	6.416	6.825	7.421	7.859	

Sources : *s* Same as for Table 4.1

area are being utilized for deployment of credit in the same area.[5] The credit deposit ratio is closely related with the economic activity prevailing in an area. Generally, economic activity and credit-deposit ratio move in the same direction. That is why, the credit-deposit ratio is usually high in developed regions/states.[6]

In Table 4.12, a synoptic view of state/region wise credit deposit ratio in India has been shown. The table shows that the credit deposit ratio in India, which stood at the 60.38 per cent in 1985, witnessed a declining trend during the later period and reached at the lowest level of 38.80 per cent in the year 2000. But, it improved and reached at the level of 48.87 per cent in 2005. Thus, the average credit-deposit ratio in India declined at a rate of 1.052 per cent during 1985-2005.

Region-wise analysis reveals that Southern Region witnessed the highest credit-deposit ratio during the years 1985-95. But, during the 2000 and 2005, Western Region enjoyed the highest credit-deposit ratio. This ratio always stood more than 75 per cent in Western Region(except 1995) and more than 66 per cent in Southern Region. On the other hand, in the North-Eastern Region, the credit-deposit ratio, which was nearly 50 per cent during 1985, declined to the lowest level of 28 per cent in 2000, but improved to 34.82 per cent in 2005.

The credit-deposit ratio witnessed a marginal increase of 0.4 per cent per annum in Western region. In all other regions it witnessed a negative growth rate during the period under context.

It is further evident from Table 4.12 that Tamil Nadu witnessed the highest credit-deposit ratio in all the years under study. This ratio always stood more than 86 per cent in Tamil Nadu. Apart from this Maharastra, Andhra Pradesh and Karnatka also witnessed more than 63 per cent credit-deposit ratio in all the years under study. In contrast to it, the credit deposit ratio stood les than 30 per cent in Arunachal Pradesh, Sikkim and Goa in all the years under context. Besides this, the national target of 60 per cent credit-deposit ratio could never be achieved in 12 states, which speaks volume about transferring of funds from these states to other parts of the country.

The credit-deposit ratio witnessed a positive growth rate

TABLE 4.12

Credit Deposit Ratio in India

(in percentage)

STATE/REGION	*1985*	*1990*	*1995*	*2000*	*2005*	*G.R.(%)*
NORTHERN	53.555	50.707	41.597	29.606	51.387	-0.206
Haryana	68.303	61.19	45.547	42.356	51.944	-1.36
Himachal Pradesh	41.521	38.573	25.969	23.755	36.029	-0.707
Jammu & Kashmir	40.793	31.788	28.62	38.457	38.633	-0.272
Punjab	45.589	45.491	41.382	39.374	45.721	0.014
Rajasthan	67.438	62.184	47.654	46.704	68.1	0.014
NORTH EASTERN	50.888	53.372	35.56	28.059	34.823	-1.879
Assam	52.358	55.518	38.683	31.99	34.395	-2.079
Manipur	71.824	69.924	58.193	37.446	40.947	-2.771
Arunachal Pradesh			12.435	15.678	24.399	6.973
Meghalaya	27.869	24.642	17.029	16.297	45.286	2.457
Mizoram			16.486	23.261	50.97	11.949
Nagaland	37.515	42.591	37.841	15.338	22.915	-2.435
Tripura	70.366	72.183	47.534	25.699	29.649	-4.229
EASTERN	50.132	52.584	47.163	37.095	46.361	-0.39
Bihar	39.802	40.035	32.502	22.455	28.896	-1.588
Orissa	86.748	81.33	54.514	41.531	62.192	-1.65
Sikkim		28.302	24.036	15.093	28.945	0.15
West Bengal	50.344	54.875	53.883	45.48	53.572	0.311
CENTRAL	50.125	52.801	39.012	33.88	40.548	-1.055
Madhya Pradesh	60.395	68.606	49.553	49.092	52.983	-0.653
Uttar Pradesh	46.468	46.998	35.098	28.196	35.438	-1.346
WESTERN	77.533	75.337	63.297	75.589	83.969	0.4
Goa			24.699	23.812	25.216	0.207
Gujarat	54.418	61.267	46.618	48.999	46.731	-0.759
Maharashtra	85.057	79.705	69.525	86.393	95.197	0.565
SOUTHERN	81.811	87.688	69.65	66.468	77.958	-0.241
Andhra Pradesh	77.215	87.148	72.971	64.235	75.094	-0.139
Karnataka	86.606	90.974	65.766	63.339	74.126	-0.775
Kerala	63.511	63.986	44.811	41.529	55.848	-0.641
Tamil Nadu	93.851	99.445	86.62	88.596	98.437	0.239
MEAN	60.381	59.398	43.119	38.804	48.867	-1.052
SD	18.847	20.782	18.637	20.22	20.741	
CV(%)	31.213	34.988	43.222	52.108	42.444	
HI(%)	5.204	5.077	4.717	5.043	4.692	

Sources : **Compsed from Table 4.4 and 4.8**

Figure-I

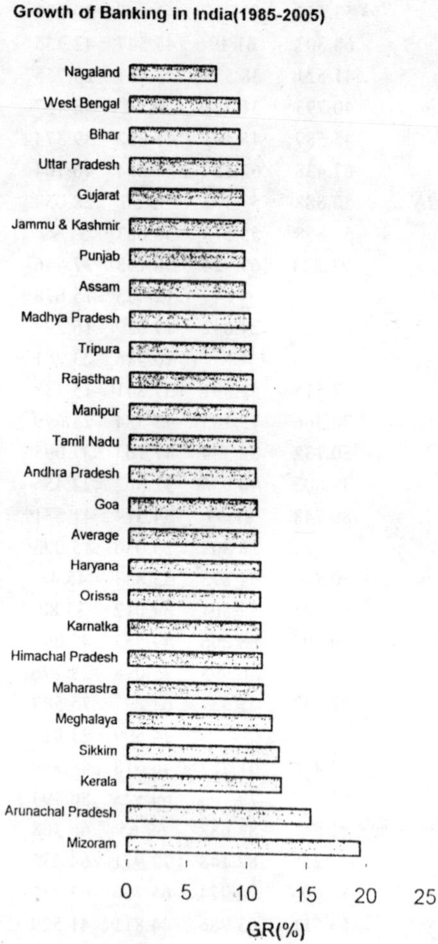

Source: Table 4.13

only in ten states during the period under study. It went up at the highest rate in Mizoram (11.949%), followed by Arunachal Pradesh (6.973%) and Meghalaya (2.457%). On the other hand, it registered the fastest decline in Tripura (-4.229%) followed by Manipur (-2.771%), Nagaland (-2.435%) and Assam (-2.079%).

In 1985 there were 11 states which witnessed more than 60 per cent credit-deposit ratio. But, the number of these states narrowed down to 5 in 2005; which shows the concentration of credit-deposit ratio in some selected states of the country. This fact is further divulged from the value of co-efficient of variation (C.V). This value was 31 per cent in 1985, but it went to 42.4 per cent in 2005.

Geometric Mean of Growth Rates of the Selected Indicators

In order to ascertain the overall growth in branch expansion, deposit mobilization and credit deployment by commercial banks in India, the geometric mean (G.M)[7] of the compound growth rates of the selected indicators have been calculated and depicted in Table 4.13. It is evident from the table that at the all India level, on an average commercial banks witnessed 10.773 per cent per annum growth rate with respect to all the banking indicators taken together.

Among the regions, Western Region (14.127%) followed by Southern (11.162%) and Northern Region (10.373%) witnessed the highest growth rate with respect to the basic banking indicators. On the other hand, Central Rregion (9.718%) followed by North-Eastern (9.754%) and Eastern Region (9.781%) showed the lowest growth rate.

A state-wise analysis reveals that Mizoram witnessed the highest growth rate (19.52%) with respect to all the banking indicators taken together (Fig.I). It was followed in descending order by Arunachal Pradesh (15.373%), Kerala (12.881%) and Sikkim (12.675%). On the other extreme, the lowest overall growth rate was witnessed by Nagaland (7.256%), West Bengal (9.183%), Bihar (9.217%) and Uttar Pradesh (9.497%). Thus, in most of the cases the low ranked states witnessed comparatively higher growth rate with respect to all the banking indicators taken together.

The inter-state variations in the growth of banking activities

TABLE 4.13
Geometric Mean of the Growth Rates of the Selected Indicators

STATE/REGION	BPA	PCD	DPA	DPB	PCC	CPA	CPB	GM
NORTHERN	***1.697***	***12.989***	***15.613***	***13.957***	***12.756***	***15.374***	***13.722***	***10.373***
Haryana	2.096	14.32	17.164	14.761	12.765	15.571	13.2	11.037
Himachal Pradesh	1.943	14.872	16.839	14.625	14.06	16.013	13.814	11.202
Jammu & Kashmir	0.708	13.422	16.255	15.416	13.113	15.939	15.102	9.6
Punjab	1.531	12.301	14.386	12.656	12.317	14.402	12.672	9.635
Rajasthan	1.25	13.25	16.152	14.713	13.38	16.285	14.844	10.351
NORTH EASTERN	***1.816***	***14.116***	***13.486***	***14.487***	***11.972***	***11.353***	***12.336***	***9.754***
Assam	1.353	14.041	15.757	14.2	11.67	13.35	11.826	9.657
Manipur	1.122	15,597	18.648	17.294	12.394	15.361	14.044	10.605
Arunachal Pradesh	--	10.199	12.848	13.013	17.884	20.717	20.894	15.373
Meghalaya	1.835	13.861	16.957	14.84	16.656	19.831	17.662	12.071
Mizoram	--	11.991	14.896	14.896	25.372	28.625	28.625	19.519
Nagaland	0.489	9.702	15.114	14.527	7.038	12.312	11.739	7.257
Tripura	1.468	15.862	18.095	16.387	10.962	13.1	11.465	10.185
EASTERN	***1.775***	***12.259***	***14.449***	***13.05***	***11.821***	***14.002***	***12.609***	***9.781***
Bihar	1.028	12.898	15.54	14.363	11.105	13.705	12.547	9.217
Orissa	1.426	15.845	17.694	16.077	13.933	15.752	14.162	11.039
Sikkim	4.381	14.63	17.915	12.989	14.802	18.092	13.159	12.675

STATE/REGION	BPA	PCD	DPA	DPB	PCC	CPA	CPB	GM
West Bengal	1.566	11.418	13.455	11.699	11.764	13.808	12.047	9.183
CENTRAL	***1.14***	***13.273***	***15.826***	***14.536***	***12.079***	***14.605***	***13.328***	***9.718***
Madhya Pradesh	1.036	13.958	16.427	15.243	13.215	15.667	14.491	10.119
Uttar Pradesh	1.175	13.004	15.597	14.254	11.484	14.042	12.716	9.497
WESTERN	***7.373***	***14.465***	***16.869***	***15.306***	***14.922***	***17.336***	***15.767***	***14.127***
Goa	1.973	13.84	15.43	13.196	14.077	15.669	13.431	10.739
Gujarat	0.932	13.371	15.656	14.572	12.511	14.779	13.7033	9.542
Maharashtra	1.377	14.652	17.098	15.485	15.299	17.759	16.137	11.293
SOUTHERN	***1.59***	***14.871***	***16.635***	***15.234***	***14.733***	***16.354***	***14.956***	***11.162***
Andhra Pradesh	1.346	14.43	16.228	14.664	14.271	16.067	14.504	10.633
Karnataka	1.181	15.671	17.641	16.257	14.775	16.729	15.356	11.052
Kerala	1.96	15.13	17.128	14.878	14.393	38.247	14.142	12.881
Tamil Nadu	1.061	14.956	16.312	15.103	15:231	16.59	15.378	10.615
Mean	**1.504**	**11.089**	**14.894**	**16.687**	**13.767**	**16.374**	**13.875**	**10.773**
CV (%)	**42.19**	**11.089**	**8.676**	**8.019**	**21.649**	**30.213**	**22.257**	**29.665**

Source : Compile from Table 4.3, 4.5, 4.6, 4.7, 4.9, 4.10 & 4.11

Note: BPA = Branches per 10,000 Sq. Kms. of Area; PCD = Per Capita Deposits; DPA = Deposits Per 10,000 Sq. Kms. of Area
DPB = Deposits Per Branch; PCC = Per Capita Credit; CPA = Credit per 10,000 Sq. Kms. of Area
CPB = Credit Per Branch; GM = Geometric Mean

in India have been assessed by calculating the co-efficient of variation (C.V) of the geometric means of growth rates of selected indicators. It is evident from Table 4.13 that the inter-state disparities stood highest (42.19%) in case of branches per 10,000 sq. kms. of area. On the other extreme the variations in the growth of banking stood the minimum (8.019%) in case of deposits per branch. By and large, the variations stood very low with respect to all the deposit based indicators and comparatively high in case of branch and credit based indicators. However the overall disparities with respect to all indicators taken together stood at a reasonably low level (29.66%) as indicated by the value of co-efficient of variation.

Composite Index of Overall Banking Development

The composite indices reflecting the state-wise level of overall banking development in India have been presented in Table 4.14. It is clear from the table that the composite indices placed Maharastra at the top in 1985 and 1990, it came down to second position in 1995 and 2000, but again succeeded to capture the first position in 2005. Similarly, Goa which stood at the top in 1995 and 2000, slid down to second position in 2005. Apart from these two states, Kerala, Punjab and Tamil Nadu also ranked high with respect to the overall index of banking development in most of the years under context. Maharastra stood at the top mainly on account of better performance with respect to deposit and credit based indicators. But, Goa managed to occupy high rank because of better performance with respect to branches and deposit based indicators(Annexure – I, II, III). On the contrary, Manipur, Tripura, Meghalaya and Assam ranked very low with respect to overall index of banking development almost in all years under study. These states ranked low because of poor performance with respect to almost all the indicators.

Classification of the States

The classification of the different states on the basis of their level of overall banking development shown in Table 4.15 reveals that Maharastra figured in the group of highly banked states throughout the period under study. Besides, Goa also figured in the category of highly banked states during 1995-2005. But, Punjab which emerged to be highly banked state in 1985 and 1990, slid

Table 4.14

Composite Indices of Overall Banking Development

	Year					
State	*1985 Index*	*1990 Index*	*1995 Index*	*2000 Index*	*2005 Index*	*Rank*
Haryana	-0.594	-1.039	-1.981	-1.349	-0.66	8
H. P.	-7.052	-7.436	-7.002	-6.306	-5.483	11
J&K	-7.403	-9.122	-7.282	-5.65	-5.795	13
Punjab	6.526	5.987	3.452	3.955	2.115	5
Rajasthan	-7.187	-8.127	-6.671	-6.053	-5.255	15
Assam	-7.629	-8.164	-7.311	-7.171	-7.049	22
Manipur	-9.57	-9.829	-7.908	-8.442	-8.168	24
Arunachal P.	--	--	-9.391	-9.005	-8.498	23
Meghalaya	-9.726	-10.319	-8.942	-8.238	-6.001	17
Mizoram	--	--	-10.313	-9.485	-7.531	19
Nagaland	-8.646	-7.907	-7.475	-8.041	-8.447	25
Tripura	-7.235	-7.121	-6.806	-7.337	-7.141	21
Bihar	-7.557	-7.724	-6.975	-6.696	-6.736	20
Orissa	-6.753	-7.461	-6.75	-6.859	-5.525	16
Sikkim	--	-2.982	-8.524	-7.517	-5.367	12
W.B.	6.229	5.678	2.203	1.638	1.234	7
M.P.	-7.826	-7.582	-6.826	-6.046	-6.072	18
U.P.	-5.304	-5.499	-5.42	-5.04	-5.094	14
Goa	--	--	11.063	13.994	11.311	2
Gujarat	-1.629	-1.448	-1.709	-1.047	-2.103	10
Maharastra	12.886	11.721	11.425	12.453	16.259	1
Andhra	-3.045	-2.988	-2.272	-2.257	-1.702	9
Karnataka	-0.798	-1.17	2.279	-0.591	1.021	6
Kerala	2.319	4.725	5.278	6.497	6.739	3
T.N.	3.224	4.414	4.475	5.207	4.993	4

Source: Computed from Annexture - I, II & III

Note: –Indicates nil.

down to the category of moderately banked states during 1995 and 2000. Due to poor performance with respect to the credit based indicator it still came down to the category of low banked states in 2005. Kerala also succeeded to occupy a place in the group of highly banked states in 1990, but in rest of the years, it remained in the category of moderately banked states. Himachal Pradesh insipte of better performance with respect to the branched based indicator slid down from the category of low banked states (during the first two years under study) to the category of very low banked states.

It is quite evident that Jammu and Kashmir, Rajasthan, Bihar, Orissa, Sikkim, Madhya Pradesh, Uttar Pradesh and all the North Eastern states continued to figure in the category of very low banked states during all the years under study. They stood in this category due to poor performance with respect to almost all the indicators.

In sum, the states with sound tourism, agricultural and industrial base ranked high with respect to the overall banking development. Though, the low ranked states succeeded to witness comparatively higher growth rates, yet they failed to come at par with the developed states.

Impact of Financial Sector Reforms On Banking in India

The banking sector reforms in India were stimulated by the report of the Committee on Financial System; popularly known as Narasimham Committee. This committee, which submitted its first report in 1991, suggested various measures to improve the efficiency and health of banking sector by making it more competitive and vibrant. On the basis of recommendations of the Narasimham Committee, commercial banks have been given much freedom to close their branches, by keeping in view their viability.

India has had more than a decade of financial sector reforms during which there has been substantial transformation and liberalization of the whole financial system.[8] It is, therefore, an appropriate time to asses the impact of financial sector reforms on various banking operations in different population groups viz. rural, semi-urban, urban and metropolitan areas.

The present section of the chapter seeks to analyse the major changes that have occurred in the banking operations of Scheduled Commercial Banks, in the wake of the banking sector

TABLE 4.15

Classification of States on the Basis of Overall Banking Development in India

Category	*Year*				
	1985	*1990*	*1995*	*2000*	*2005*
Highly Banked	Punjab, Maharastra	Punjab, Maharastra, Kerala	Goa, Maharastra	Goa, Maharastra	Goa, Maharastra
Moderately Banked	W.B, Kerala, T.N	W.B, T.N	Punjab, Karnataka, Kerala, T.N	Punjab, Kerala, T.N	Kerala, T.N
Low Banked	Haryana, Gujarat, H.P., Andhra, Karnataka	Haryana, Gujarat, H.P., Andhra, Karnataka	Haryana, W.B, Gujarat, Andhra	Haryana, W.B, Gujarat, Andhra Karnataka	Haryana, Punjab W.B. Gujarat. Andhra Karnataka
Very Low Banked	J&K, Rajasthan, Assam, Manipur, Meghalaya, Nagaland, Tripura, Bihar, Orissa, M.P, U.P	J&K, Rajasthan, Assam, Manipur Meghalaya, Nagaland, Tripura, Bihar, Orissa, M.P, U.P, Sikkim	H.P, J&K, Rajasthan, Assam, Manipur Arunachal Pradesh Meghalaya Mizoram, Nagaland Tripura, Bihar, Orissa, Sikkim, M.P., U.P.	H.P, J&K, Rajasthan, Assam, Manipur Arunachal Pradesh Meghalaya Mizoram, Nagaland Tripura, Bihar, Orissa, Sikkim, M.P., U.P.	H.P, J&K, Rajasthan, Assam, Manipur Arunachal pradesh Meghalaya Mizoram Nagaland, Tripura Bihar, Orissa, Sikkim. M.P., U.P

Source : Computed on the basis of Table 4.14.

Note : W.B- West Bengal, T.N-Tamil Nadu, Pb.-Punjab H.P-Himachal Pradesh, J&K-Jammu & Kashmir M.P-Madhya Pradesh, U.P-Uttar Pradesh.

LEVEL OF BANKING DEVELOPMENT IN INDIA : 2005

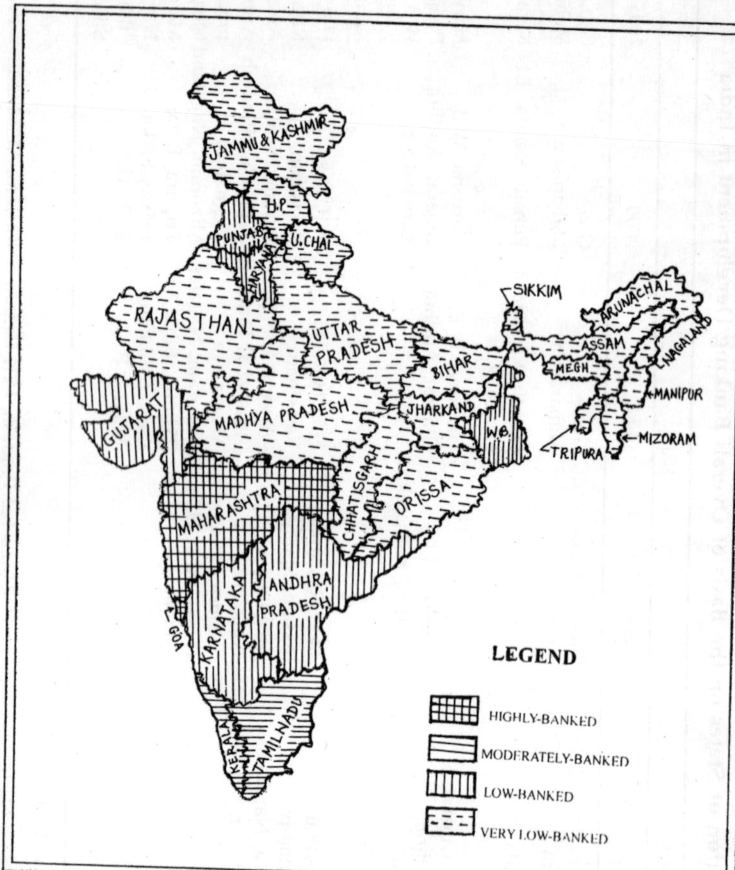

Source : Drawn on the basis of Table 4.15

reforms in India.. The analysis has been carried out at three points of time i.e for the year 1982, 1992 and 2005, to analyse the changes in banking operations during the pre-reform (1982-92) and post reform (1992-2005) period.

Population Group-Wise Branch Expansion

The total number of Scheduled Commercial Bank branches in India went up from 40.79 thousand in 1982 to 60.69 thousand in 1992 and further to 68.12 thousand in 2005 (Table 4.16). It is evident that the pace of growth in the number of branches decelerated considerably during the post reform period as compared to the previous one.

TABLE 4.16

Population Group-Wise Distribution of Bank Branches in India (No.)

Pop. Grp.	*Year* 1982	1992	2005	*GR (%) (1982-92)*	*GR (%) (1992-2005)*
Rural	21626 (53)	35218 (58)	31958 (47)	5.00	-0.74
Semi Urban	8921 (22)	11397 (19)	15375 (22)	2.48	2.33
Urban	5511 (13)	8285 (14)	11498 (17)	4.16	2.55
Metro.	4735 (12)	5790 (9)	9285 (14)	2.03	3.70
Total	40793 (100)	60690 (100)	68116 (100)	4.05	0.89

Source : Same as for Table 4.1.

Note : Figures in parentheses show the percentage in total.

During the pre-reform period (1982-92), the number of branches witnessed the highest growth rate in rural areas (5.00%), followed by urban (4.16%) and semi-urban areas (2.48%). On the contrary, during the post reform period whereas on the one hand the number of branches went up at the highest rate of 3.7 per cent per annum in metropolitan areas, in rural areas they came down at a rate of 0.74 per cent per year.

The bane of the financial system as it has grown during the 1990s is that it has been increasingly becoming urban-centric. It is evident from the table that the proportion of rural branches in total scheduled commercial bank branches in India, was 53 per cent in 1982 which went up to 58 per cent in 1992. But, after the RBI gave up its bank expansion programme w.e.f 1st April, 1995, the number of rural branches of scheduled commercial banks has steadily come down. As a result, the share of rural branches declined from 58 per cent in 1992 to 47 per cent in 2005. In contrast to it, the metropolitan areas registered an opposite trend in their bank branches. Their share in total branches declined from 12 per cent to 9 per cent during the pre-reform period, but upsurged to 14 per cent during the post reform period.

Thus, the pre-reform policy of spreading bank network in unbanked and rural areas, seems to have been given up in the wake of the banking sector reforms. Such an operational change is sure to hurt the process of providing institutional credit to rural areas in general and unbanked areas in particular. Moreover, the national policy of growth with equity(personal as well as regional) is likely to suffer a setback if the bank branches in far flung rural areas are closed on the consideration of their viability.

Population Group-Wise Deposit Mobilisation

Deposit mobilization by Commercial Banks is important from the standpoints of expansion of resources of banks, inculcating the habit of thrift on the part of the public and channelisation of resources for the development planning of the country. Table 4.17 brings into light that total bank deposits in India went up almost at the same rate during the pre as well as post financial sector reform period.

The population group-wise analysis of data reveals that whereas the rate of deposit mobilization came down in rural areas, it picked up in all other areas during the post-reform period as compared to the previous one. It is further evident that the percentage share of rural areas in total deposit mobilization went up marginally from 14 per cent to 15 per cent during 1982-92, but again came down to 12 per cent in 2005. The semi-urban and urban areas also showed a declining trend in their percentage share in total deposits, throughout the period under reference.

But, in sharp contrast to it, the proportion of deposits mobilized by scheduled commercial banks from metropolitan areas, which was 38 per cent in 1982 increased considerably to 42 per cent in 1992 and further to 50 per cent in 2005.

TABLE 4.17
Population Group-Wise Deposits of Commercial Bank in India

(Rs. crore.)

Pop. Grp.	*Year* 1982	1992	2005	*GR (%) (1982-92)*	*GR (%) (1992-2005)*
Rural	7414 (14)	35058 (15)	213536 (12)	16.81	14.91
Semi Urban	11977 (23)	45869 (20)	296303 (17)	14.37	15.43
Urban	12990 (25)	53892 (23)	376133 (21)	15.29	16.12
Metro.	19900 (38)	98266 (42)	867201 (50)	17.32	18.24
Total	52280 (100)	233086 (100)	1753173 (100)	16.12	16.79

Source : Same as for Table 4.1.

Note : Figures in parentheses show the percentage in total.

Population Group-Wise Credit Deployment

Credit deployment by scheduled commercial banks at the all India level picked up from 14.83 per cent per annum to 17.5 per cent per annum during the post reform period as compared to the earlier period(Table 4.18). It is worth to notice that whereas on the one hand, the rate of growth of credit deployment slowed down considerably in rural areas it picked up in all other areas particularly in metropolitan areas, during the post reform period.

It further comes into light that the proportion of credit deployed in rural areas went up marginally from 13 per cent in 1982 to 14 per cent in 1992, but sharply came down to 9 per cent in 2005. On the contrary, the proportion of credit deployed in metropolitan areas went up from 49 per cent to 50 per cent during 1982-92 and further sky-rocketed to 63 per cent in 2005. Thus, during the post reform period, metropolitan areas enjoyed credit at the cost of rural, semi-urban and even urban areas.

TABLE 4.18

Population Group-Wise Credit of Commercial Banks in India

(Rs. crore)

Pop. Grp.	*Year*			*GR (%) (1982-92)*	*GR (%) (1992-2005)*
	1982	*1992*	*2005*		
Rural	4473 (13)	20587 (14)	106497 (9)	16.49	13.48
Semi Urban	6114 (17)	21779 (15)	130596 (12)	13.55	14.77
Urban	7577 (21)	29268 (21)	189593 (16)	14.47	15.46
Metro.	17515 (49)	70578 (50)	731121 (63)	14.95	19.70
Total	35679 (100)	142211 (100)	1157807 (100)	14.83	17.50

Source : Same as for Table 4.1.

Note : Figures in parentheses show the percentage in total.

Population Group-Wise Credit-Deposit Ratio

The credit-deposit ratio is also a good indicator reflecting the performance of banking sector. This ratio reveals that how much part of the deposits mobilized from a particular area is deployed in the form of credit in the same area[9]. In India, the credit-deposit ratio of scheduled commercial banks which was 68 per cent in 1982, declined to 61 per cent in 1992, but again improved to 66 per cent in 2005.

The population group-wise analysis of data reveals that rural, semi-urban as well as urban areas witnessed a negative growth rate in credit deposit ratio both during the pre and post reform period. But, during the post reform period the decline has been much sharper in rural areas. In contrast to it, in metropolitan areas the credit-deposit ratio though came down from 88 per cent to 72 per cent during 1982-92, but again shot up to 84 per cent in 2005.

TABLE 4.19

Population Group-Wise Credit-Deposit Ratio in India

(in %age)

Pop. Grp.	*Year*				
	1982	*1992*	*2005*	*GR(%) (1982-92)*	*GR(%) (1992-2005)*
Rural	60	59	50	-0.22	-1.27
S-Urban	51	47	44	-0.81	-0.51
Urban	58	54	50	-0.71	-0.59
Metro.	88	72	84	-1.99	1.19
Total	68	61	66	-1.08	0.61

Source : Computed from Table 4.17 and Table 4.18

This kind of trend in credit-deposit ratio is very disquieting when viewed against the direction of RBI to commercial banks to maintain at least 60 per cent credit-deposit ratio in rural and semi-urban areas. Moreover, it speaks volume about transferring of resources mobilized from rural to metropolitan areas.

Inter-State Disparities in Banking Development

The inter-state disparities in the growth of banking activities in twenty five major states of India(reflected by the values of co-efficient of variation), narrowed down with respect to all the indicators during the pre-reform period(Table 4.20). On the other hand, during the post reform period, the inter-state disparities though narrowed down in case of deposit mobilization, yet they widened further in case of credit deployment. It has happened because of the fact that whereas on the one hand, the public sector banks have slowed down their banking activities in rural areas, on the other hand, foreign and private sector banks have given a thrust to the so called 'high street commercial banking' in metropolitan areas.

TABLE 4.20
Inter-State Disparities with respect to Different Banking Indicators

(C.V. %)

Indicator	*Year* 1982	1992	2005
PPB	52	30	42
BPA	118	96	90
PCD	109	97	96
DPA	145	130	125
PCC	96	78	95
CPA	127	112	120

Source : Same as for Table 4.1
Note : PPB = Population Served Per Branches.
BPA = No. of Branches Per 10,000 Sq. Kms. of Area.
PCD = Per Capita Deposits.
DPA = Deposits Per 10,000 Sq. Kms. of Area.
PCC = Per Capita Credit.
CPA = Credit Per 10,000 Sq. Kms. of Area.

TABLE 4.21
Values of Coefficient of Variation and other Variables with respect to Population Based Indicators

Indicator Variable.	*Population Served Per Bank Branch ('000)*			*Per Capita Deposits (Rs.)*			*Per Capita Credit (Rs.)*		
	1982	*1992*	*2005*	*1982*	*1992*	*2005*	*1982*	*1992*	*2005*
Mean X	20.57	13.55	16.48	651	2829	16032	338	1318	7891
S.D.	10.81	4.12	7.0	710	2748	15343	324	1027	7525
C.V (%)	52	30	42	109	97	96	96	78	95

Source : Same as for Table 4.1

Thus, whereas the banking sector reforms have been successful in improving the health and efficiency of the banking industry in India, they have failed grossly in achieving the objective of growth with equity. In this context, it is important to recognize

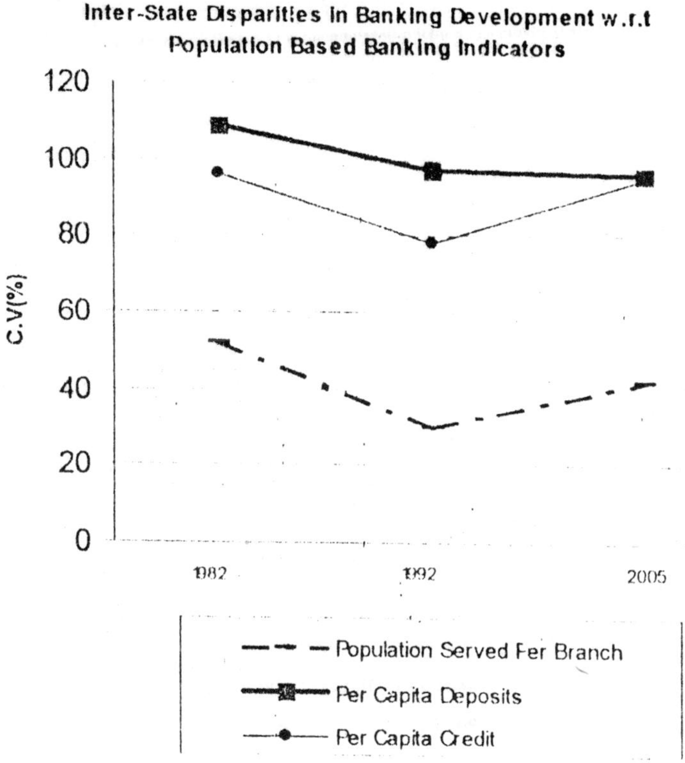

Figure - II

TABLE 4.22

Values of Coefficient of Variation and other Variables with respect to Area Based Indicators

Indicator Variable.	*No. of Branches Per 10,000 Square Kms. of Area*			*Deposits Per 10,000 Square Kms. of Area (Rs. Crs.)*			*Credit Per 10,000 Square Kms. of Area(Rs. Crs.)*		
	1982	*1992*	*2005*	*1982*	*1992*	*2005*	*1982*	*1992*	*2005*
Mean (X)	156	222	254	174	850	5895	97	419	3040
S.D.	184	213	227	253	1109	7377	123	471	3634
C.V (%)	118	96	90	145	130	125	127	112	120

Source : Same as Table 4.1

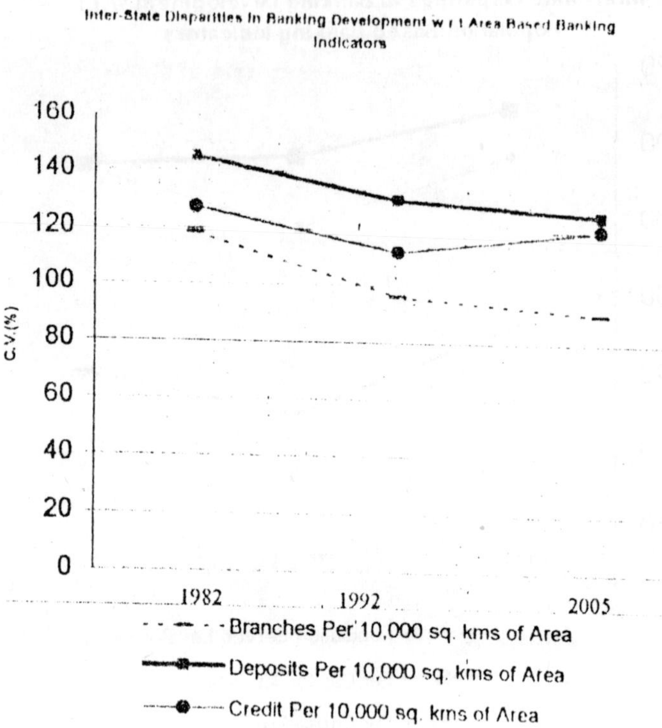

FIGURE III

that in the emerging global economic scenario there is no way out but to expose the domestic public sector banks to competition(domestic as well as foreign). But, privatization in no way is the ultimate panacea to infuse efficiency in public sector banks. In fact, it is important to keep in mind that excessive competition may create an unstable banking environment, while insufficient competition may breed inefficiency or reduce credit access for the needy borrowers.

NOTES AND REFERENCES

1. H.L. Sharma, *Commercial Banking Development - A study of Himachal Pradesh*, Rajat Publications, New Delhi, 2003, p. 87.

2. S.N. Ghoshal and M.D. Sharma, *Economic Growth and Commercial Banking in a Developing Economy*, Scientific Book Agency, Calcutta, 1965, p. 74.

3. Meenakshi Soodan, ***Regional Disparities of Commercial Banking in India***, Kanishka Publishing House, Delhi, 1992, p. 96.

4. H. L. Sharma, "Need to Boost Banking in Himachal Pradesh", ***Yojana***, Vol. 37, No. 17, Sept 30, 1993, p. 26.

5. C. Rangarajan, ***Innovations in Banking***; Oxford and IBH Publishing Co., New Delhi, 1982, p. 42.

6. H.L. Sharma, ***Commercial Banking Development - A study of Himachal Pradesh***, Rajat Publications, New Delhi, 2003, p. 103.

7. The geometric mean (G.M) is defined as the nth root of the product of all the 'n' values of a variable. Symbolically;

$$G.M. = (X_1.X_2.X_3....X_n)^{1/n} = \text{Antilog}\left[\frac{\Sigma \text{ Log } X}{n}\right]$$

8. Rakesh Mohan, "Financial Sector Reforms in India : Policies and Performance Analysis", ***Economic and Political Weekly***, Vol. XL, No. 12, March 19-25, 2005, p. 1106.

9. H.L. Sharma, "Regional Rural Banks in Himachal Pradesh", ***Kurukshetra***, Vol. XLIV, No. 10, July 1996, p. 42.

5

SUMMARY AND SUGGESTIONS

CONCLUSION

The developing countries like India face glaring disparities in their economic development. These disparities have become the most serious problem in the path of their economic development. To reduce these disparities the balanced regional development of banking sector is most compulsory.

Balanced economic development of a country implies economic development of all regions. But, it does not imply that the rates of growth and level of development of all regions should be equal. It simply means that difference in the economic development of different regions should be minimum. But, inspite of more than five decades of economic planning, the regional pattern of growth in India is far from being balanced one. Here a few states are relatively more developed and many others are economically backward. In this context, the commercial banks are expected to play a pivotal role by financing the requirements of agriculture, industry, trade and commerce in the desired direction. Of late, the concept of banking has enormously undergone a change from merely accepting of deposits and granting of credits. They are now considered the catalytic agents of development.

A number of research studies have been conducted in India on various aspects of commercial banking development. Most of these studies are confined to the analysis of quantitative and qualitative changes taking place in Indian banking during pre-reform period. Whereas, some of the studies are solely concerned with the allocative aspects of commercial banks, others attempt to analyse the regional variations in the growth of banking in India. The review of literature reveals that with some exceptions, no comprehensive and systematic study have been carried out to critically analyse the inter-state disparities in the development of commercial banking, particularly in the wake of the new banking policy which departs fundamentally from the traditional banking policy.

India has had more than a decade of banking sector reforms during which there has been a substantial transformation and liberalization of the whole banking system. It is therefore, an appropriate time to take stock of the situation and assess the adequacy and efficacy of our approach.

The present study endeavors to analyse the extent and direction of regional disparities in commercial banking development in India, during the year 1985, 1990, 1995, 2000 and 2005. The scope of study is confined to scheduled commercial banks only. The specific objectives of the study are: (i) to analyse the extent and direction of inter-state disparities in banking activities in India, (ii) to examine the impact of financial sector reforms on banking in India, and (iii) to identify the backward states with respect to banking development in India. The level of banking development in different states have been measured with the help of nine indicators based on branch expansion, deposit mobilization and credit deployment. In order to assess the growth in banking activities compound growth rate have been calculated. The extent and nature of inter-state disparities with respect to the selected indicators has been measured with the help of co-efficient of variation and Herfindahl Index. Further, in order to find out the level of banking development and extents of variations with respect to all the indicators taken together, the composite indices have been constructed with the help of Z-Sum Technique. Finally, the states have been classified into four categories namely; highly-banked, moderately-banked, low-banked and very-low-banked, on the basis of the composite scores obtained by the states.

The analysis brings into light that the scheduled commercial bank branches in India went up at a marginal rate of 0.418 per cent per annum during the reference period. As a result of very slow pace of branch expansion the population served per branch also went up from 14.6 thousand in 1985 to 16.5 thousand in 2005. On account of low growth rate in branch expansion, the number of branches per 10,000 sq. kms. of area also went up at a low rate of 1.5 per cent per annum. On the basis of the branch based indicators Goa, Kerala, Punjab and Himachal Pradesh ranked high in most of the years. On the contrary, Manipur followed by Nagaland, Arunachal Pradesh and Madhya Pradesh ranked the lowest with respect to these indicators.

A key achievement by commercial banks in India has been the high growth rate in deposits despite the slow down in branch expansion during the post reform period. Their deposits went up nearly 20 times registering a growth rate of 16.4 per cent per annum during the reference period. As a result of an impressive increase in deposit mobilization in the country, deposits measured in relation to population, geographical area and branches, also went up at a rate of more than 14 per cent per annum. On the basis of deposit based indicators; Goa, Maharastra, Punjab and Kerala ranked high in most of the years under study. On the other hand; Manipur, Mizoram, Orissa and Madhya Pradesh ranked the lowest in almost all the years.

The commercial banks showed better performance not only in deposit mobilization but with respect to credit deployment also. The analysis points out that the total credit deployment in the country witnessed the growth rate of 16 per cent per annum, as a result of which credit per 10,000 sq. kms. of area also went up at the same rate (16 %). Credit per branch and per capita credit also went up at a rate of more than 13 per cent per annum during the period under study. On the basis of credit based indicators; Maharastra followed by Tamil Nadu always stood at the top. On the other hand, Arunachal Pradesh, Meghalaya, Nagaland and Sikkim ranked very low with respect to credit based indicators.

An evaluation of the emerging banking scenario in India brings into light that whereas the pace of branch expansion slowed down during the post reform period (1992-2005), it picked up in case of credit deployment. The proportion of rural areas in total number of bank branches as well as in deposit mobilization and credit deployment declined during the post reform period as compared to the earlier one. But, the metropolitan areas registered a high increase in their percentage share in total branch expansion, deposit mobilization and credit deployment.

The credit deposit ratio witnessed a decline in all types of population groups (except metropolitan areas) during post financial sector reform period. In metropolitan areas, this ratio though declined from 68 per cent to 61 per cent during 1982-1992,but again went up to 66 per cent in 2005.This type of trend in credit-deposit ratio indicates that there has been a shift of resources to metropolitan areas from other areas.

The study brings into light that in most of the cases the difference between low ranked and high ranked states widened further over a period of time. As a result, the inter-state disparities with respect to all the indicators went up in 2005 as compare to 1985.The variations stood at a high and alarming level with respect to banking indicators in relation to area as compare to population based banking indicators.

On the basis of composite indices of banking development Maharastra emerged to be highly banked state in all the years under study. Besides this, Goa also occupied a place in the category of highly banked states during the period 1995-2005. Punjab figured in the category of highly banked states during 1985 and 1990. But, due to poor performance with respect to credit based indicators it slid down to the category of low-banked states in 2005. On the other hand, Jammu & Kashmir, Rajasthan, Bihar, Orissa, Sikkim, Madhya Pradesh, Uttar Pradesh and all the North-Eastern states emerged to be very-low-banked in all the years under study. They stood in this category due to poor performance with respect to almost all the indicators.

SUGGESTIONS

The scheduled commercial banks in India have acquired a wide reach, judged in terms of expansion of branches, growth of deposits and credit. The objective of banking policy has been translated into reality in operational terms to considerable extent in the country. The massive expansion of banking activities in rural, semi-urban and low-banked areas has been made possible only due to controlled banking. This would have remained a distant dream, had the banking industry been remained in the private sector. The gains of nationalization can further be consolidated only if no major reversal takes place in the present status of commercial banks. A reversal from nationalization may no doubt, yield some short term economic benefits. However, its social cost is likely to be far greater.

Presently, the pre-reform policy of spreading bank network in unbanked and rural areas, seems to have been given up in the wake of banking sector reforms. Such an operational change is sure to hurt the process of providing concessional credit to weaker sections of the society located in rural areas in general and unbanked areas in particular. Moreover, the national policy of growth with equity (personal as well as regional) is likely to suffer a set back if the bank branches in far flung rural areas are closed on the consideration of their viability.

Though the targets of branch expansion, to large extent have been achieved, yet doubts do arise about the quality, efficiency and effectiveness of this spread. In fact, the banking infrastructure should not be judged in a narrow sense of measuring the number of branches in terms of population served per branch or coverage of geographical area. Rather, it should also be judged from the quality, efficiency and effectiveness of the services provided by the banks. If the motivation of the staff working in rural areas is to be further improved, more deposits are to be mobilized and rural development is to be achieved, banking in rural areas has to be redefined in wider rather than narrow sense.

The unprecedented branch expansion has resulted in some organizational problems too. Shortage of staff and their reluctance to serve in remote and rural areas, have created problems of managing the rural branches. There is usually lack of communication between rural branches and their controlling offices located in the urban areas. Due to lack of proper coordination and cooperation among different tiers of the banking structure, the gains of branch expansion are not properly exploited. Beside this, there has to be rural orientation of the banking staff working in rural areas. Unless they become a part of the rural society they can not deliver the goods efficiently.

Over the years, though the bank deposits have shown a

phenomenal increase, yet it is not commensurate with rate of increase in money supply. This could be probably due to large scale investments in corporate equities, mutual funds and in many new schemes of Unit Trust of India (UTI), Life Insurance Corporation (LIC) and other non-banking financial institutions having tax incentives. Such a constraint on the growth of investible resources will adversely affect the profitability of commercial banks. Further more, the non-banking financial companies (NBFCs) which were of only marginal significance in the pre-reform period, have today come to occupy a prominent position. They are expected to snatch a large share of deposits from the banks. To cope up with such growing competition, the commercial banks should diversify their activities to augment their profitability. It is important to have such a framework for banks that their operational flexibility is maintained on a sustainable basis. Banks will have to be less rigid in their operations. Moreover, there is the need for adequate measures to be taken to make the bank deposits more attractive and lucrative, failing which they will be unable to discharge the social responsibility casted upon them.

It is important to ensure competitive banking for rural areas, so that the masses have a choice of alternative banking channels and efficient banking services. A greater play of autonomy to restore efficiency, productivity and profitability is also required. The banking sector reforms initiated in 1991, broadly directed a gradual reduction in statutory pre-emption of resources of banks, rationalization of their interest rate structure and the prescription of the prudential norms. These measures are meant to improve the allocation and financial efficiency of the banking system.

Banks are confronted with a number of problems with respect to credit deployment also. High proportion of loans given under priority sector, has poised the problem of poor recovery rate and huge overdues with adverse consequences on banks' income through concessional interest rate and high administrative cost of such loans. At this stage, the credit system should not be overburdened with excessively detailed specification of targeted lending and interest rate concessionality. Rather, the specific requirements of the really needy should find recognition.

Credit deployment of commercial banks can be made effective by improving banking awareness and banking habits among the rural masses through the mass media. In the low-banked states, with greater involvement of the banks and by educating the people about the details of the schemes available, the gains of banking can be enhanced.

The present criteria of classifying different regions into rural and semi-urban areas also suffers from a severe limitation. Treating areas with a population of 10,000 or less as rural areas, results in the inclusion of even small towns in this category. As a result, the concessional credit facilities which are basically intended for the upliftment of the rural masses, are in fact availed of by the people leaving in small towns also. The same holds good in case of semi-urban areas as well. Thus, it would be desirable to have a more realistic criterion for classification of population, even if the number of categories increases.

It is also desirable to have further concessional credit schemes for tribal, draught prone and hilly areas, as these regions deserve special attention for their speedy development.

Last but not least, the banking sector reforms have been successful in improving the health and efficiency of the banking industry in India, they have failed grossly in achieving the objective of growth with equity. In this context it is important to recognize that in the emerging global economic scenario there is no way out, but to expose the domestic public sector banks to competition (domestic as well as foreign). But, privatization in no way is the ultimate panacea to infuse efficiency in public sector banks. In fact, it is important to keep in mind that excessive competition may create an unstable banking environment, while insufficient competition may breed inefficiency and reduce credit access for the needy borrowers.

Summary of the Findinds

The developing countries like India face glaring disparities in their economic development. These disparities have become the most serious problem in the path of their economic development. To reduce these disparities the balanced regional development of banking sector is most compulsory.

The present study endeavors to analyse the extent and direction of regional disparities in commercial banking development in India, during the year 1985, 1990, 1995, 2000 and 2005. The scope of study is confined to scheduled commercial banks only. The specific objectives of the study are: (i) to analyse the extent and direction of inter-state disparities in banking activities in India, (ii) to examine the impact of financial sector reforms on banking in India, and (iii) to identify the backward states with respect to banking development in India. The level of banking development in different states have been measured with the help of nine banking indicators. The extent and nature of inter-state disparities with respect to the selected indicators has been measured with the help of co-efficient of variation and Herfindahl Index. Further, in order to find out the level of banking development and extents of variations with respect to all the indicators taken together, the composite indices have been constructed with the help of Z-Sum Technique. Finally, the states have been classified into four categories, on the basis of the composite scores obtained by the states.

The analysis brings into light that scheduled commercial bank branches in India, went up at a marginal rate of 0.418 per cent per annum during the period under study. As a result of very slow pace of branch expansion, the population served per branch also went up from 14.6 thousand in 1985, to 16.5 thousand in 2005. A key achievement of the commercial banks in India has been the high growth rate of deposit mobilization and credit deployment, despite the slow down in branch expansion during the post reform period. The total deposits as well as total credit of the commercial banks in the country went up at a rate of more than 16 per cent per annum during the reference period.

The analysis points out that in most of the cases the difference between low ranked and high ranked states widened further over a period of time. As a result, the inter-state disparities with respect to all the indicators went up in 2005 as compared to 1985. The variations stood at a high and alarming level with respect to banking indicators in relation to geographical area as compared to population based banking indicators.

The study brings into light that the proportion of rural areas in total number of bank branches as well as in deposit mobilization and credit deployment declined during the post reform period as compared to the pre-reform period. But, the metropolitan areas registered a high increase in their percentage share in total branches, deposit mobilization and credit deployment. The credit-deposit ratio witnessed a decline in all types of population groups(except metropolitan areas) during the post financial sector reform period. But, in metropolitan areas, this ratio though declined from 68 per cent to 61 per cent during 1982-92, but again went up to 66 per cent in 2005.

On the basis of composite indices of banking development, Maharastra and Goa emerged to be highly banked states in all the years under study. On the other hand, Jammu & Kashmir, Rajasthan, Bihar, Orissa, Sikkim, Madhya Pradesh, Uttar Pradesh and all the North-Eastern states emerged to be very low-banked states in all the years under study. They stood in this category due to poor performance with respect to almost all the banking indicators.

ANNEXURES

Annexure - I

Composite Indices of Branch Expansion

State	*1985*	*1990*	*1995*	*2000*	*2005*
Haryana	-2.794	-3.003	-2.789	2.325	-1.816
H. P.	-3.752	-3.948	-3.637	-3.251	-2.841
J&K	-4.164	-4.494	-4.148	-3.737	-3.307
Punjab	-1.856	-2.177	-2.071	-1.561	-1.107
Rajasthan	-3.878	-4.167	-3.855	-3.45	-3.035
Assam	-3.612	-3.829	-3.523	-3.159	-2.784
Manipur	-4.195	-4.512	-4.128	-3.723	-3.321
Arunachal Pradesh	--	--	-4.281	-3.867	-3.439
Meghalaya	-4.011	-4.31	-3.924	-3.529	-3.114
Mizoram	--	--	-4.138	-3.733	-3.312
Nagaland	-4.126	-4.441	-4.1-8	-3.71	-3.285
Tripura	-3.549	-3.793	-3.449	-3.094	-2.709
Bihar	-2.864	-3.122	-2.898	-2.552	-2.19
Orissa	-3.675	-3.948	-3.627	-3.237	-2.832
Sikkim	--	-0.951	-4.029	-3.603	-3.131
W.B.	-2.008	-2.023	-1.867	-1.543	-1.235
M.P.	-3.847	-4.114	-3.82	-3.427	-3.026
U.P.	-2.807	-3.027	-2.839	-2.478	-2.102
Goa	--	--	-0.598	0.138	0.543
Gujarat	-3.378	-3.68	-3.414	-3.024	-2.643
Maharastra	-3.365	-3.627	-3.364	-2.936	-2.555
Andhra Pradesh	-3.422	-3.71	-3.434	-3.024	-2.612
Karnataka	-3.08	-3.383	-3.151	-2.737	-2.339
Kerala	0.065	-0.371	0.244	0.633	1.066
Tamil Nadu	-2.458	-2.741	-2.546	-2.158	-1.833

Source: Computed from Table 4.2 and 4.3

Note: -- Indicates nil.

Annexure - II

Composite Indices of Deposit Mobilisation

State	*1985*	*1990*	*1995*	*2000*	*2005*
Haryana	0.545	0.941	0.219	0.425	0.523
H. P.	-0.725	-0.702	-0.8	-0.779	-0.786
J&K	-0.603	-0.975	-0.742	-0.568	-0.723
Punjab	5.871	5.915	2.833	3.087	2.017
Rajasthan	-2.12	-2.275	-1.633	-1.725	-1.963
Assam	-1.808	-2.182	-1.744	-1.84	-1.666
Manipur	-3.337	-3.287	-2.503	-2.515	-2.312
Arunachal P.	--	--	-0.917	-1.644	-1.661
Meghalaya	-1.428	-1.483	-1.243	-1.383	-1.352
Mizoram	--	--	-2.079	-2.602	-2.42
Nagaland	-1.222	-0.903	-1.382	-0.928	-1.622
Tripura	-2.463	-2.387	-1.946	-1.655	-1.544
Bihar	-1.567	-1.537	-1.635	-1.396	-1.599
Orissa	-2.78	-2.826	-2.108	-2.098	-2
Sikkim	--	1.178	-1.349	-0.58	0.04
W.B.	5.179	4.58	1.097	1.475	1.131
M.P.	-2.163	-2.296	-1.803	-1.842	-1.782
U.P.	-0.934	-0.644	-0.914	-0.694	-0.922
Goa	--	--	8.477	10.194	9.092
Gujarat	1.345	1.13	0.698	0.612	0.62
Maharastra	6.08	6.294	4.895	4.197	6.208
Andhra Pradesh	-0.782	-1.092	-0.987	-0.878	-0.737
Karnataka	-0.4	-0.624	3.168	-0.28	0.401
Kerala	2.393	2.264	1.966	2.837	2.376
Tamil Nadu	0.621	0.909	0.435	0.579	0.684

Source: Computed from Table 4.5, 4.6 and 4.7

Note: -- Indicates nil.

Annexure - III

Composite Indices of Credit Development

State	*1985*	*1990*	*Year* *1995*	*2000*	*2005*
Haryana	1.655	1.023	0.589	0.551	0.633
H. P.	-2.575	-2.786	-2.565	-2.276	-1.856
J&K	-2.636	-3.653	-2.392	-1.345	-1.765
Punjab	2.511	2.249	2.69	2.429	1.205
Rajasthan	-1.189	-1.285	-1.183	-0.878	-0.257
Assam	-2.209	-2.153	-2.044	-2.172	-2.599
Manipur	-2.038	-2.03	-1.277	-2.204	-2.535
Arunachal P.	--	--	-4.193	-3.494	-3.398
Meghalaya	-4.287	-4.526	-3.775	-3.326	-1.535
Mizoram	--	--	-4.096	-3.15	-1.799
Nagaland	-3.298	-2.563	-1.985	-3.403	-3.54
Tripura	-1.223	-0.941	-1.411	-2.588	-2.888
Bihar	-3.126	-3.065	-2.442	-2.748	-2.947
Orissa	-0.298	-0.687	-1.015	-1.524	-0.693
Sikkim	--	-3.209	-3.146	-3.234	-2.276
W.B.	3.058	3.121	2.973	1.906	1.338
M.P.	-1.816	-1.172	-1.203	-0.777	-1.264
U.P.	-1.863	-1.828	-1.667	-1.868	-2.07
Goa	--	--	3.184	3.662	1.676
Gujarat	0.404	1.102	1.007	1.365	-0.08
Maharastra	10.171	9.054	9.894	11.192	12.606
Andhra Pradesh	1.159	1.814	2.149	1.645	1.647
Karnataka	2.682	2.837	2.262	2.426	2.959
Kerala	-0.139	2.832	3.068	3.027	3.297
Tamil Nadu	5.061	6.246	6.586	6.786	6.142

Source: Computed from Table 4.9, 4.10 and 4.12

Note: -- Indicates nil.

BIBLIOGRAPHY

BOOKS

Abrol, Prem Nath, ***Commercial Banking***, Anmol Publishers, New Delhi, 1987.

Aggarwal, B.P., ***Commercial Banking in India***, Classical Publishing Company, New Delhi, 1981.

Bhagwati, Jagdish and Padma Desai, ***India : Planning for Industrialisation***, OUP, London, 1970.

Bhattacharya, B.N., *Regional Behaviour of Bank Deposits and Its Implications to Deposit Mobilisation*, (Mimeo), National Institute of Bank Management, Pune, 1985.

Bilgrami, S.A.R., ***Growth of Public Sector Banks – A Regional Growth Analysis***, Deep & Deep Publications, New Delhi, 1982.

Campbell, Colin D. and Rosemary Campbell, ***An Introduction to Money and Banking***, The Dryden Press Hinsdale, Illions, New Hampshire, 1981.

Chawla, A.S., ***Nationalisation and growth of Indian Banking***, Deep & Deep Publications, New Delhi, 1987.

Chhipa, M.L., ***Commercial Banking Development in India***, Printwell Publishers, Jaipur, 1987.

Decay, W.M., ***The British Banking Mechanism***, London, 1960.

Desai, Vasant, ***Indian Banking, Nature and Problems***, Himalaya Publishing House, Bombay, 1979.

Dhingra, Ishwar. C., ***The Indian Economy : Environment and Policy***, Sultan Chand and Sons, New Delhi, 2002.

Dreze, J. and Amartya Sen, ***Indian Economic Development and Social Opportunity***, Oxford University Press, New Delhi, 1996.

________________, ***India : Development and Participation***, Oxford University Press, New Delhi, 2002.

Edward, W. Bood, ***Commercial Bank Management***, Harper & Row, New York, U.S.A., 1964.

Garg, S.C., ***Indian Banking Cost and Profitability***, Anmol Publications, New Delhi, 1989.

Ghoshal, S.N. and M.D.Sharma, ***Economic Growth and Commercial Banking in a Developing Economy***, Scientific Book Agency, Calcutta, 1965.

Government of India, ***Report of the Committee on Banking Sector Reforms***, (Chairman : M. Narasimham), GOI, New Delhi, 1998.

_________, ***Report of the Committee on the Financial System***, (Chairman : M. Narasimham), Ministry of Finance, GOI, New Delhi, 1991.

_________, ***Report of the Working Group on Revival of Weak Public Sector Banks***,(Chairman : M.S. Verma), GOI, New Delhi, 1999.

Hamson, J. and S. Kathuria, ***India : A financial Sector for the Twenty First Century***, Oxford University Press, New Delhi, 1999.

Hugar, S.S. (ed.), ***Trends and Challenges to Indian Banking***, Deep & Deep Publications, New Delhi, 1993.

Husain, Farhat, ***Public Sector Commercial Banking in India***, Deep & Deep Publication, New Delhi, 1986.

Jhingan, M.L., ***Money Banking and International Trade***, Konark Publications, New Delhi, 1986.

Kalkundrikar, A.B., ***Regional Rural Banks and Economic Development***, Daya Publishing House, New Delhi, 1990.

Kindleberger, C.P., ***Economic Development***, Mc Graw Hill Book Company, Inc., New York, 1965.

Mahajan, V.S. (ed.), ***Studies in Indian Banking and Finance***, Vol. 1, Deep & Deep Publications, New Delhi, 1989.

Meier, G.M., ***Leading Issues in Economic Development***, Oxford University, Press, New York, U.S.A., 1984.

Myrdal, Gunnar, ***Economic Theory and Underdeveloped Regions***, Vohra & Company, Bombay, 1958.

Nayyar, R., ***Rural Poverty in India : An Analysis of Inter-State Differences***, Oxford University Press, New Delhi, 1992.

Negi, Bhupal Singh, ***Co-operative Credit and Regional Development***, Deep & Deep Publications, New Delhi, 1990.

Prashad, K.N., ***Indian Economy Since 1951 : Growth With Imbalance***, Intellectual, New Delhi, 1993.

Rangarajan, C., ***Innovations in Banking***, Oxford and I.B.H. Publishing Co., New Delhi, 1982.

Rao, Hemlata, ***Regional Disparities and Development in India***, Ashish Publishing House, New Delhi, 1984.

Rao, V.V.K., and Subrahmanyam; ***Development of Andhra Pradesh : 1956-2001 – Study of Regional Disparities***, NRR Research Centre, Hyderabad, 2002.

Reddy, Y.V., ***Monetary & Financial Sector Reforms in India***, UBS, Delhi, 2000.

Reed, E.W., ***The Commercial Bank Management***, A Harper International Student Reprint, 1964.

Sayers, R.S., ***Modern Banking***, Oxford University Press, London, 1951.

Sharma, B.P., ***The Role of Commercial Banks in India's Developing Economy***, S. Chand and Company Ltd., New Delhi 1974.

Sharma, H.L., ***Commercial Banking Development***, Rajat Publications, New Delhi 2003.

Sharma, H.L., ***Nationalisation of Banks in India – Retrospect & Prospect***, Sahitya Bhawan, Agra, 1991.

Shekhar, K.C., ***Banking Theory and Practice***, Vikas Publishing House Pvt. Ltd., New Delhi, 1979.

Singh, Ajit, ***Rural Development and Banking in India***, Deep & Deep Publications, New Delhi, 1985.

Singh, S., ***Performance Budgeting for Commercial Banks in India***, The Macmillan Company of India Ltd., Delhi, 1977.

Singha, Ajit Kumar, ***New Economic Policy of India***, Deep & Deep Publications, New Delhi, 1994.

Sooden, Meenakshi, ***Regional Disparities of Commercial Banking in India***, Kanishka Publishing House, New Delhi, 1992.

Srinivasan, R., ***Priority Sector Lending : A Study of Indian Experience***, Himalaya Publishing House, Bombay, 1995.

Subrahmanya, Susheela and M.V.S. Gowda,(eds.), ***Regional Economic Development in India***, Deep & Deep Publications, New Delhi, 1995.

Vashist, A.K., ***Public Sector Banks In India***, H.K Publishers and Distributors, New Delhi, 1991.

Vyas, M.R., ***Financial Performance of Rural Banks***, Arihant Publishers, Jaipur, 1991.

PAPERS AND ARTICLES

Adi, Mukta S., "Need to Stem Inter-State Disparities", ***Yojana***, Vol. 45, June 2001, pp. 7-14.

Ahuja, Kanta, "The Banking Sector After the Reforms", ***The Indian Economic Journal***, Vol. 44, No. 4, April-June, 1997, pp. 1-18.

Angadi, V.B., "Bank Advances to Priority Sector- An Enquiry into the Causes of Concentration", ***Economic and Political Weekly***, Vol. XVIII, No. 13, March 26, 1983, pp. 503-10.

Avari, Dara, D., "Reforms in Banking", ***The Indian Economic Journal***, Vol. 41, No. 4, April-June 1994, pp. 13-19.

Bhatia, B.S. and A.S. Chawla, "Banking and new Economic Programme," in S.D. Tripathi and K.K. Uppal(eds.), ***Banking and New Economic Programme***, Publication Bureau, P.U. Chandigargh, 1984.

Borkar, D.G., "Development of Bank Credit", ***Financial Express***, March 25, 1992, p. 27.

Chhipa, M.L. & Sushma Sagar, "Banking Development in India : A Study in to the causes of Regional Differentials", ***Prajnan***, Vol. X, No. 4, October-December 1981, pp. 371-77.

Chhipa, M.L., "Rural Banking Development Pattern of Scheduled Commercial Banks in India", ***Prajnan***, Vol. XV, No. 1, January-March 1986, pp. 49-64.

Dadibhavi, R.V., "Regional Variations in Financial Infractural Development in India", ***Prajnan***, Vol. XVI, No. 4, October-December 1988, pp. 391-408.

Das, Abhiman, et. al., "Liberisation, Ownership and Efficiency in Indian Banking – A Nonparametric Analysis", ***Economic and Political Weekly***, Vol. XL, No. 12, March 19-25, 2005, pp. 1190-97.

Devi, P. Ambiga, "Regional Disparities in Banking Development in Tamil Nadu – 1991", ***The Indian Economic Journal***, Vol. 44, No. 2, October-December, 1996, pp. 143-46.

Ghosh, D.N., "Commercial Banking : Lessons from Indian Experience", ***The Journal of the Indian Institute of Bankers***, Vol. LX, No. 1, January-March 1989, pp. 45-51.

Giri, A.K. & Tamal Dasgupta, "Some Aspects of Inter-State and Intra-State Variations in the Flow of Institutional Agricultural Credit", ***Indian Journal of Agriculture Economics***, Vol. 43, No. 3, July-September, 1988, pp. 364-73.

Goiporia, M.N., "Credit Policy and its Impact on Economic Activity in India", ***The Banker***, Vol. XXXII, No. 2, April 1985, pp. 27-29.

Haque, T. & Sunita Verma, "Regional and Class Disparities in the Flow of Agricultural Credit in India", ***Indian Journal of Agriculture Economics***, Vol. 43, No. 3, July-September 1988, pp. 356-63.

Jadhav, N. and D. Ajit, "The Role of Banks in Economic Development of India", ***Prajnan***, Vol. XXV, Nos. 3-4, October 1996 – March 1997, pp. 309-19.

Kannan, R., "Banking Development and Regional Disparities",

The Indian Economic Journal, Vol. 35, No. 2, July-September 1987, pp. 58-76.

Kannan, R., "Banking Development and Regional Disparities", *The Indian Economic Journal*, Vol. XXXV, No. 2, July-September, 1987, pp. 58-76.

Kohli, Renu, "Directed Credit and Financial Reforms", *Economic and Political Weekly*, Vol. XXXII, No. 42, October 18-24, 1997, pp. 2667-76.

Krishan, Bal, "Role of Commercial Banks in Removing Regional Banking Disparities in Rural India", *Prajnan*, Vol. XVI. No. 2, April-June 1987, pp. 145-51.

Krishna, Raj, "The Centre and the Peripheri – Inter-State Disparities in Economic Development" in Choudhary, Gamkar & Ghosh(eds.) *The Indian Economy and its Performance Since Independence*, OUP, Delhi, 1990.

Kundu, Amitbah et.al. "Regional Disbution of Infrastructure and Basic Amenities in Urban India", *Economic & Political Weekly*, Vol. XXXIV, No. 28, July 10, 1990.

Mahajan, V.S., "Public Sector Banks Lose Shine", *Financial Express*, Vol. XIX, No. 145, July 21, 1993, p. 7.

Mallya, P.D., "Performance Management System in Banks", *Prajnan*, Vol. XXXII, No. 3, October-December 2003, pp. 243-253.

Manju, A.B., "Banks Pip the Posts on Efficiency", *Financial Express*, Vol. XXIII, No. 65, April 22, 1997, p. 4.

Mathur, Ashok, "Regional Economic Change and Development Policy in India", in K. Puttaswamaiah(ed.), *Economic Policy and Tax Reforms in India*, Indus, New Delhi, 1994.

Mohan, Rakesh, "Financial Sector Reforms in India : Policies and Performance Analysis", *Economic and Political Weekly*, Vol. XL, No. 12, March 19-25, 2005, pp. 1106-21.

Mohan, T.T. and Subhash C. Ray, "Comparing Performance of Public and Private Sector Banks – A Revenue Maximisation Efficiency Approach", *Economic and Political Weekly*, Vol. XXXIX, No. 12, March 20-26, 2004, pp. 1271-76.

Murthy, Y. Sree Rama & G. Haresh, "Regional Variations in Banking Business : A Study Based on ANOVA Technique", ***Prajnan***, Vol. XX, No. 1, January-March 1991, pp. 31-43.

Murthy, Y.S.R. and G. Haresh, "Regional Variations in Banking Business : A Study Based on ANOVA Technique", ***Prajnan***, Vol. XX, No. 1, January-March, 1991, pp. 31-43.

Nagarajan, N., "Commercial Banks in Non Traditional Areas," in Hugar S.S. (ed.) ***Trends and Challenges to Indian Banking***, Deep & Deep Publications, 1993, pp. 121-75.

Narasimham, M., "Banking Sector Reforms : The CSF Report and After", ***Prajnan***, Vol. XXV, No. 3-4, October 1996-March 1997, p. 221.

Narasimham, M., "Financial Sector Reforms", in Ajit K. Singha (ed.), ***New Economic Policy of India***, Deep & Deep Publications, New Delhi, 1994, pp. 350-66.

Oka, G.S., "Agricultural Advances of Commercial Banks, 1973-81", ***Reserve Bank of India Bulletin***, Vol. XXXIX, No. 9, September 1985, pp. 646-63.

Padmanabhan, K., "Lead Banking and District Credit Plan : A Case Study" in V.S. Mahajan(ed.), ***Studies in Indian Banking and Finance***, Deep & Deep Publications, New Dehli, 1989.

Panagariya, Arvind, "Growth and Reforms During 1980s and 1990s", ***EPW***, XXXIV, No. 25, June 19-25, 2004, pp. 2581-94.

Panda, J. & P.K. Sahu, , "Changing Pattern in the Growth of Commercial Banking in India", ***The Indian Journal of Commerce***, Vol. 36, No. 137, December 1983, pp. 80-94.

Parihar, R.S. and N. Singh, "A Study into Institutional Finance for the Agricultural Sector in

Punjab", ***Indian Journal of Agriculture Economics***, Vol. 43, No. 3, July-September, 1988, pp. 381-89.

Patel, A.R., "Development North-Eastern Region Through Banking", ***Yojana***, Vol. 32, No. 21, November 16-30, 1988, pp. 19-21.

Patel, K.V. and D.P. Khankhoje, "Rural Banking : Basic Issues and Scope for Restucturing", ***Prajnan***, Vol. XXI, No. 4, January-March, 1993, pp. 455-74.

Paul, R.C., "The Role of Banking in the New Economic Programme", in J.D. Tripathy and K.K. Uppal(eds.), ***The Role of Banking and the New Economic Programme***, Publication Bureau, Punjab University, Chandigarh, 1984.

Prasad, Sharda, "Role of Banks in a Developing Economy" in P.D. Hajela(ed.), ***Role of Commercial Banking in a Developing Economy***, Popular Prakashan, Bombay, 1969.

Qazi, Moin, "Banks and Rural Development", ***The Banker***, Vol. XXXI, No. 10, December 1984, pp. 37-40.

Rangarajan, C., "Banking with the Poor", ***Reserve Bank of India Bulletin***, Vol. XLVII, No. 2, February 1994, pp. 353-56.

Ratnan, N. Vijay, "Commercial Banks and Mass Banking – Myth or Reality", ***Yojana***, Vol. 27, No. 13, July 16-31, 1983, pp. 19-20 & 34.

Ravisankar, T.S., "Towards Structural Changes in Banking", ***Prajnan***, Vol. XXI, No. 4, January-March, 1993, pp. 439-53.

Sahu, Gagam Bihari and D. Rajasekhar, "Banking Sector Reforms and Credit Flow to Indian Agriculture", ***EPW***, Vol. XL, No. 53, December 31, 2005-January 6, 2006, pp. 5550-59.

Sarker, P.C., "Management of Regional Imbalances in Regional Development of India : Graphical Approach", Reserve Bank of India Occasional Papers, Vol. 10, No. 1, March 1989, pp. 1-37.

Sarma, Rudra Sen, "Cost and Profit Efficiency of Indian Banks During 1986-2003 – A Stochastic Frontier Analysis", ***Economic and Political Weekly***, Vol. XL, No. 12, March 19-25, 2005, pp. 1198-1208.

Saroja, S., "Stoppers on Bank Branch Expansion?",***Financial Express***, Vol. XIX, No. 124, June 30, 1993, p. 7.

Shah, R.C., "Restructuring the Banking System in India", ***Prajnan***, Vol. 10, No. 2, April-June, 1981, pp. 135-49.

Sharma, H.L., "Changing Commercial Banking Scenario in India – An Analysis", paper presented in UGC Sponsored National Seminar on, "Banking and Insurance Sector Changing Economic Scenario : Challenges and Responses", Organised by D.A.V College Jalandhar, on November 21st & 22nd , 2005.

__________, "Financial Sector Reforms in India-Challenges Ahead", paper presented in U.G.C. sponsored Regional Seminar on, "Economic Reforms and Their Impact on the Indian Economy", Organised by Deptt. of Economics, Govt. College Dharamshala, during October 14-15, 2005.

__________, "Need to Boost Banking in Himachal Pradesh", ***Yojana***, Vol. 37, No. 17, Sep. 30, 1993, pp. 25-26.

__________, "Regional Rural Banks in Himachal Pradesh", ***Kurukshetra***, Vol. XLIV, No. 10, July 1996, pp. 41-44.

__________, "Structural Adjustment in Trade Policy", in G. S. Batra and Narender

Kaur(eds.), ***Indian Economic Policy***, Anmol Publications, New Delhi, 1995, pp. 79-99.

Sharma, H.L. and Meenakshi Sooden, "Growth of Commercial Banks in Himachal Pradesh", paper presented in the National Seminar on Development Alternatives for Underdeveloped Areas of India – Social Science Perspective, Organised by Deptt. Of Economics, H.P.U, Shimla, during 24-25 April, 2000.

Sharma, H.L. et. al., "Impact of Financial Sector Reforms on Banking in India", paper presented in AICTE sponsored National Seminar on, "Service Sector Management", Organised by, Regional Institute of Management and Computer Technology(RIMT), Mandi Gobindgarh, Punjab. during March 9-11, 2006.

Sooden, Meenakshi, "Inter-State Disparities of Commercial Banks in India", ***Prajnan***, Vol. XXVI, No. 2, 1997-98, pp. 143-58.

Sreedharan, M., "The Indian Banking Industry's Dilema", ***Express Investment Week***, Vol. 6, No. 51, December 16-22, 1996, pp. 10-13.

Srivastava, T.N., et. al., "Disparities in Deployment", ***The Economic Times***, April 26, 1990, p. 11.

Sugayya, N., "Performance of Scheduled Commercial Banks in Andhra Pradesh : An Evaluation", ***Prajnan***, Vol. VIII, No. 2, April-June 1979, pp. 205-21.

Tarapore, S.S., "An Assessment of Indian Economic Reforms", ***Prajnan***, Vol. XXV, No. 3-4, October 1996-March 1997, p. 239.

Vaish, M.C. & M.L. Chhipa, "Factors Affecting Regional Commercial Banking Development in India", ***Prajnan***, Vol. XVI, No. 3, July-September 1988, pp. 279-99.

Varde, S.D., "On the Dimensions of Disparities in Banks' Branch Network", ***Prajnan***, Vol. VI, No. 1, January-March 1977, pp. 25-40.

Wali, M.M.K., "Institutional Credit for the Rural Poor", ***The Indian Journal of Public Administration***, Vol. XXVI, No. 3, July-September, 1980, pp. 710-24.

Yerram, B. Raju, "New Role for Commercial Banks in Agricultural Credit", ***Prajnan***, Vol. V, No. 1, January-March, 1976.

__________, "Restructuring Public Sector Banks Imminent", ***Financial Express***, Vol. XX, No. 77, May 12, 1994, p. 6.

Journals, Magazines and Dailies

American Economic Review

Commerce

Economic and Political Weekly

Economic Review

Economic Times

Express Investment Week

Financial Express

Indian Co-Operative Review

Indian Economic Journal

Indian Journal of Agriculture Economics

Indian Journal of Commerce

Indian Journal of Economics

Indian Journal of Public Administration

Journal of Indian Institute of Bankers

Kurukshetra

Link

Lok Udyog

Prajnan

Reserve Bank of India Bulletin

The Banker

The Capital

The Tribune

Times of India

Yojana

INDEX